Divine Spirituality

Getting To Know The Real You

Osiris Akkebala

iUniverse, Inc.

New York   Bloomington

iUniverse books may be ordered through booksellers or by contacting:

*iUniverse
1663 Liberty Drive
Bloomington, IN 47403
www.iuniverse.com
1-800-Authors (1-800-288-4677)*

*ISBN: 978-1-4401-7605-0 (sc)
ISBN: 978-1-4401-7604-3 (ebook)*

Printed in the United States of America

iUniverse rev. date: 10/23/2009

Book Cover Marketing Statement For Divine Spirituality

REVELATION, beyond research, Divine Spirituality takes you on a journey revealing to you Divine Information that can not be footnoted, GOOGLE searched, nor found in dictionaries, libraries, and bibles. Dare to take the journey that will reveal the knowledge of your Divine self.

The Beauty Of Love

Oh my dear, the power of my love for you,
Blind me from the illusion I see, as it
Equip me with the ability to envision the
True beauty of your soul.

The beauty of love linger in my Mind for
You, causing me to doubt not your love and
Do assure our happiness among the company
Of the stars.

Can it be that heaven gate has open for me
And there within, your beauty glow, as the
Countenance of your face truly show,
Assuring me of the love I see.

Such is the beauty of love that should always be and come
to me in an expression of Divine Spirituality.

©2005 By Osiris Akkebala

Dedication

Without the two people that have made this book possible, Divine Spirituality would not have been written and to them I am eternal grateful.

The two people are

Tawnya Mitchell (daughter)

Haadiya Aamon, also selected the Divine Spirituality Book design.

To these two people I am forever indebted to for keeping me focus while writing this most profound book.

To them I say, Thank You.

Author, Osiris Akkebala

About The Author

Osiris is a Hierophant Spiritualist a scribe who records Divine Information that comes from revelations, who through remote viewing channeling, receives Divine Information. He has the Mental qualities, that far exceed the contemporary method of belief concerning God, Universe, and Self, he is formerly a Ordained Baptist Minister who has Pastored several churches. He has earned a AA degree in political Science, and a BA degree in Sociology, a diploma in Executive management. He is a Divine Spiritual teacher with a Divine Knowledge of the Divine Body Life, who has traveled extensively both physical and mentally.

Osiris Akkebala is an ordain former Baptist Minister who have has been the pastor of several churches and he is a teacher of the Ancient mysteries gleaned from the Ancient Pyramid Texts.

Osiris today does not associate himself with any Religion, organized or other wise. Osiris is a Spiritual Master Teacher, who receive the information that he share from using the Mental process of Channeling and Remote Viewing and from every day life experiences and he constant Meditate on the Ancient Ancestors for Divine Guidance.

Osiris is a graduate from the University Of Central Florida with a B A degree in Sociology with a Minor in Political Science, with studies in Humanities, Philosophy, Ethic and Education.

Osiris is a Divine Spiritual man, he is a conscious and dedicated Father to eight children and several Grand and great Grand Children.

Osiris live in Orlando Florida though he has had the experience of Traveling extensively over the course of his distinguish Life.

Osiris has had the pleasure of visiting Afrika, Great Britain and Switzerland as well as many states in the United States and a visit to the Bahamas.

Osiris has appeared on several National Talk Shows.

Osiris is a Lecturer, Public Speaker and Teacher on the subject of Divine Spirituality, Religion, and Socio/political issues.

Osiris is one that can command your attention when speaking on the Divine Attributes of the Mind.

Osiris can be reached for Lecturers, Speaking engagement, by simply dialing these numbers to book Osiris or to speak to the Author.

The Best Book of the new millennium to serve as a Mental guide to discovering your Divine Spirituality, the Discover of the Real You, Osiris Akkebala Revelation will inspire the reader of this book to desire to discover the meaning and power of the Divine Mind, the Mind that will cultivate your spirit to become exposed to the life of Joy, freedom, guided with a Mind that introduce you to a dimension that is beyond the realm of consciousness.

Osiris bravely go where no man has gone before to have you to explore the real you, a depth of Mind that is not hindered by vain Ego, Envy, and Jealousy, but by the Divinity of your Intuitive Conscious, a Dimension of the Body life that extend beyond the dimension of the conscious and unconscious level of the Body Life, where vain belief does not reside in the domain of your Divine Spirituality.

Your Divine Spirit is the guide to you, that will eliminate all of the uncertainty about the Divine Essence, (GOD) both Universe, and more personal, about Thyself.

Osiris reveal how the Mind is the key to living a peaceful life with justice being its companion for us all, and how by our belief, we have been misguided in believing in all of the profane things in life, never knowing what constitute the spirit of our life and what it will take to involve ourselves with the Divine Spirit of our Being, a Spirit that consist of Life Attitude and Behavior.

Profoundly written with creative revelation, come this most powerful and revealing book about the Real You, Guided by Your Divine Spirituality.

Divine Spirituality is an exhilarating and provocative book, written under the guidance of Spiritual obedience to the Soul, the intuitive Energy Intelligence of the Divine Essence

Osiris is a Hierophant with Divine Mental qualities, who far exceed the contemporary method of belief concerning God, Universe, and Self, he is a Divine Spiritual teacher with a Divine Knowledge of the Divine Body Life, who has traveled extensively both physical and Mentally.

To take this Divine Spiritual journey, you the reader have a decision to make for Thyself.

I acknowledge the DIVINE LESSONS that CHIEF ELDER OSIRIS have been is continuous to feed the entire family with. I have benefited much from all the DIVINE LESSONS. I can draw strength to carry on. I hereby recommend HIS DIVINE LESSONS TO ANYONE TO STUDY AND FEED THEIR DIVINE EXISTENCE.... NDIFOR ANKHHORUS NGWA... Finland

The eloquent, the Divine, the raw wisdom and the blunt truth are the words, the enlightening (for many) messages of Chief Elder Osiris missives. I've known him since I was in my 20's now, and what a ground he is and/or can be for any live wire and no matter their physical or mental age either. He is many things, as any one in-tuned is... He is a writer indeed as well, but a Divine man first and one of few who places all karmic energy into the message to all people, and of Divine consciousness of the soul into the ever-presence of Universal existence. These are the inevitability's stressed by this man rather than the "play the game" process of thought in order to position himself into a more glamorous yet blinding light. He can be of envy to any of his peers, as many children have been abandoned and let down and an inspiration for my own peers in my young age because this old man has obviously not sold his soul, which only means to compromise the Divine mind that is Divinely designed to mirror the soul... Kevin D. Ervin author of "The Journey Continues into the Never-ends."

In every generation, we are honored to have a person in our midst who can connect us to our Divine Spirituality. This Author is not interested in a populous or a self serving message. This author is not willing to accept partial or negotiated freedom for us all. He will never make deals that would limit your potential to be and act like the people we all are equipped to be.

We are at the crossroads of historical Time and our very survival depends on our return to expressing and revealing our Divine Spirituality.

This author is not a political assignment. This author is not a religious assignment, this author is one of moral and spiritual correctness and as you read this book, I am sure that you the reader will form the same opinion about the author as I have had the honor to form my opinion, which I am sharing in this, my acknowledgment of this book and the author.

We as people need to look no further than the work and words of our esteemed and Divine Spiritual Elder, Chief Elder Osiris Akkebala, and it is my honor to acknowledge his place among us and as the author who is in our midst today, sharing his revelation about Divine Spirituality.

Thank You
Author of:
I MUST LET MY PEOPLE KNOW
Dalani Aamon-CEO & Founder
The Harambee Radio & Television Network

It is with great humility I write this acknowledgment of Osiris Akkebala, who I know affectionately as Chief Elder.

Some years ago I had the good fortune to become aware of this man who has tirelessly worked on behalf of the mind liberation of people world wide. He has served in many capacities, as Minister, Political pundit, Spiritual Leader and Guide. My encounter with Chief Elder in Cyber-space so many years ago, lead to my having the great honor of meeting him in person.

Chief Elder, is a man of great patience, a man who is Divinely guided, I thank him for his dedication and tireless work on our behalf. He is a visionary who's Spiritual eye has seen us in our Divine state and continues to share his love and devotion with us and consistently delivers the message in his writings of that which we are destined to be once again. I look forward to reading his new book.

Thank you Chief Elder
Sista, Ngon'e Ada Aw

There is no other book that stimulates your mind, spirit and soul as this book does.

Divine Spirituality is a book clearly written from divine revelations because of the **indepth-ness** that it delves into on topics of Meta Physics and Spirituality in a way that has never been broken down before.

There are profound new terms when explaining very difficult explanations and interpretations of how we as Divine beings (not human beings as stated by the author) are direct relatives of the universe and the elements and how both of these entities are the ingredients of what we are made of and should live our lives according to the laws that governs them.

It is a fascinating time traveling, mind blowing read. As you read you will find out that the terms that we have been taught by way of religio such as doing things and loving from your heart isn't speaking of your physical heart. Many of us don't realize that the heart is just an organ and is not the place where emotions and feelings come from   This book goes blow for blow connecting you to how our physical, Mental and Spiritual Beings have become separated but yet how and what we must do to bring them to function as one again. How they should function and why they're not functioning with the Meta Physical world of the unseen and the physical world that we think we see   My favorite characteristic of this book and the author is how he goes on to explain a very complex topic and picks it up again and again until you get it, it is beautifully written in yet another new term that I describe as "Meta Physical Poetry".

There are some terms when speaking metaphysically that the human language have not the words for which is another clarification that this Masterpiece, "Divine Spirituality" was not thought out by a human mind and is indeed divine revelations.

goddess Kalif
aka Tawnya Mitchell

Contents

Introduction

Many have written on the topic of spirituality, but this book introduce you to Divine Spirituality, A Spirituality that deal with the Mind-Sense relationship, a relationship that qualify you to get to know the meaning and purpose of the Mind to Sense relationship.

This book reveal to you the Divine meaning of Spirit-Spirituality, which is entirely different from the conventional distorted meaning most of us have been conditioned to believe about what constitute the Spirit of the body, and when you are not in the know of what the Spirit actually is, then the Mind in incapable of producing a Divine Spirit to cause your life to experience a Divine Spiritual life.

This book, Divine Spirituality: Getting To Know The Real You, take you on a journey of Divine proportion that will allow you to venture into chambers of Mind Thought that will for the first Time have you getting to know the real you.

This book, Divine Spirituality: Getting To Know The Real You, deal with every aspect of the Body Life Function, using the Mind to be your Guide, a Mind that must come to be Divine, that is if the desire of the reader is to be able to understand what Divine Spirituality is all about, and is capable of qualifying you to take one of the most internal journey into the Soul Revelation of your Life.

Divine Spirituality: Getting To Know The Real You, cover every aspect of the Soul, Body, Mind, Spirit, Conscious, Beyond Conscious, and into the Intuitive Dimension of the Body Soul of your Being, which reveal to you how you are to experience your Divine Spirituality.

This book dare you to venture inside of you, where you will get to know the Real You, this is a book, once you begin to read it, then you will not be able to not finish it, so take the dare and read this book, Divine Spirituality: Getting To Know The Real You, You Won't Regret That You would Have Made a most Divine Decision to read this most Divine Enlightening Book about your Body Mind, Divine Spirituality.

Divine Reading

The Author
Osiris Akkebala

Divine Spirituality

Preface

This is not a book about religion, even though religion will be mention in this book, this is a book about you the people of the world, regardless of Race, Creed, or Religion.

This book is about your Divine Spirituality, it is about the Divine Essence, which is the infinite Energy Intelligence that produced and revealed us all To Be.

In this book, it will indicate that there was neither a premeditated agenda nor a command of expectation coming from the Divine Essence (GOD) to all things that has been produced by the Divine Essence. (GOD)

All that the Divine Essence produce is Divine, and I must say that many of us have morph to become the antithesis to our Divinity, and now have come to subscribe to projecting a spirit that is referred to as being Evil.

Such is what prompt me to share with you indicating to you what the Divine essence has produced, has the freedom of choice in making the decisions that will be made that will effect your life.

An evil spirit is not natural to the Divine Essence original production, it is the evil spirit that has come to be by its own belief about God and self, as it is in many of us who no longer express a Divine spirit in the world today, so now many in the world today express a spirit toward each other that is not of Divine quality.

In dealing with spirituality you have two methods of spiritual expression, one is a esoteric display of spiritual character and the other is a display of exoteric expression, the former being expressed by a well defined close secretive group, whose expression is in harmony, order, and balance, which is a display of the inner expression of the ethereal Divine self, the self that extend beyond the physical self.

The esoteric behavior is an act by a chosen few to learn about the mental ability that can cause you to know about things that can be learned esoterically, it been done acting in secrecy, meaning all that it is done and said esoterically and is kept to memory.

So the information that is coming solely from the inner intuitive self action is not coming from the mental action of the physical self but it is expressed in a very divinely spiritual way, exoterically.

Yet when dealing with the exoteric spirit of your body life, it is about the outer expression, revealing the quality of your spirit, which can be defined as being a public display of your body life action, open so all can be aware of your spirit.

Your spirit is expressed by you and it is what reveals your mind action, expressed by an inner locking of your sense to mind performance, which is the way the spirit is expressed by you.

Therefore, the spirit is no more than a display of your attitudinal behavior, demonstrated by the performance of your body life action.

It is your mind that is most compelling when revealing the quality of spirit that is demonstrated by your body life, which is an indication of the quality of mind that is guiding your body life.

As always, life is physical and during the course of your life living it require a Divine Mind to express a Divine Spirit and it is such a mind that is capable of taking you inward beyond the mind horizon into the ethereal dimension of your intuitive informative self, which I intend to reveal more about later.

There is nothing natural about evil, it is an acquired behavior which now has become an evolved part of life Human Beings DNA, something the Divine Essence played no part in producing.

Because you must see, it is the Energy of Divine Perfection that is absent of evil, so evil does not reside in a Divine Being, which you started out with the Mind that caused you to be Divine.

It is the active spirit of the Divine Energy Essence (GOD) that is incapable of producing evil, so our life fall from our Divine state of being, is our doing, so all that happen in our lives, we have only ourselves along with those acting evil toward you, to blame.

There was a Time when all that is, was Divine in its behavior toward each other, and now the world has evolved and revolved to become capable of expressing evil by becoming Human Beings who once was with a higher order of Divine intelligence.

But now has come to become Human Beings that are influenced in making the choices now being made in your life while you are claiming to have freedom of will in your lives.

So here you are with a need to strive to regain your Divine Spirituality and now it is evil that has come to be a part your lives and evil is the only action that is preventable from causing you to become once again the type of world that once was Divine in expressing the Divine nature that was common to the first world.

So, this is a book speak freely and has no inhibition in sharing the Divine Truth with you the reader and it do so without conforming to the status quo present body life living condition of the Human Being today.

It is the Nature of the Human Beings we have evolved to become today, a Human Being capable of acting evil in a world that once was Divine in expressing its Spirituality.

This is a book that will reveal information that will be counter too much you have been taught concerning God, Universe, and the nature of being your Divine Self.

 I will delve into the so call unknown as well as the known as it has been told to you, but the difference will be that I will not share with you information on the topics I will cover in this book that is common to you, which will not be based on what you have been led to believe about the topics that will be addressed in this book.

The Divine revealed information in this book has come from beyond the Physical senses of believing and has been revealed from the Metaphysical Esoteric Dimension, an existential of the Mind action that is not govern by the Body conscious ability to perform.

 so this will be a Mind journey into the abyss of Divine institutive self where the Divine Truth and Reality is revealed to you, which has nothing to do with your ability to Think / believe.

So in order to be capable of comprehending what this book will reveal about the Divine Essence and about the God of the Human Being and the Esoteric Universe, as well as the Exoteric Universe, then you must be willing to learn about the Human Being Self and about Spirituality, which is expressed Divinely as well as Profanely, if not, then you must not open this book, because to do so, you must open it with a virgin Mind.

So much in the form of Lies have come to you regarding God, Universe, and your Spiritual Self, each being told to you in the way it is not, and most Time, when the topic of Spirituality is written about, all of such information has a common theme, which is Religion.

In actuality the information you are given about the Spirit of the Being and the Various so call Spiritual Dimension of Metaphysical Esoteric Travel, is of that which is based upon a Religious belief concerning a Religious God.

This book will not spare your religious teaching of belief concerning God, Soul, Spirit, and Mind, as so been established by people referring to themselves as Human Beings.

Such a classification of a Being, has been Produced by the Divine Essence, many now in power, now serve to contradict the Natural Character of the Living Being, which I refer to as being a Divine Being.

Divine Beings are those who once used the Divine Mind to Think have gone to become a Profane Human Being, those Beings who now confess not to have ever been Perfect in the activity of the Body Life living.

Life is a Gift given by a Perfect Entity of Action, which I refer to as the Divine Essence of all Beings (God) and they are all Things that Live, be they Animate or inanimate, in and out of the nature of Life, be it in Motion or is Immutable.

This Book is about exploring the inner self, the past life of yourself, back there where the Divine truth reveal all that need to be known about your life.

It will explore the mental capability of you, your body life consisting of the soul, mind, and spirit.

 So I urge you to enjoy the book, because it is going to take you on a journey of Mental proportion where you have never been before, so let you begin.

Definition

(A.) Divine Essence (God)- Can not be defined, must be acknowledged, having the same rank as God, but is of a different mental Dimension and Is the Energy Power that cause all things to be physical and Metaphysical.

(B) Soul- (Energy) The Life of the body, the Divine Energy within your self, from which all Divine information about all things are revealed to the Body- Mind.

(C) Body- the Life physical temple that house the Metaphysical World, it being the Soul, mind, Spirit Life.

(D) Brain- The body instrument that is subject to the Soul, it is that which give the Body, a sign of Life, both physical and Mental.

(E) Mind- The recorder of thought, an ethereal entity of the Soul Energy made to be manifest by the body ability to Think, receiving information to be expressed Mentally and physically, a nonphysical entity of the body from which all information of and in the Mind is stored and revealed.

(E) Spirit- the attitudinal behavioral expression of the Mind, through body expression.

(F) Metaphysical - the nonphysical of the Esoteric Ethereal World, the inner domain of your body self.

(G) Meditation- the mental interaction with the esoteric world, thoughtless travel into the Metaphysical Dimension.

(H) Divine-Mind, Spirit, Body interaction in harmony, order and balance.

(I) Profane- Mind, Spirit, Body interaction in disharmony, disorder, and imbalance.

(J) Religion- a Doctrinal set of Rules and Commands Of God, consisting of symbols, metaphors and allegories created by mankind.

(K) Charka- Energy Points of the body where energy is assemble to cause a harmonic rhythmic action that enhance life meaning to the body, those points being the brain, heart, stomach, pelvic.

(L) Esoteric- Information shared with a few, about nonphysical happening occurring in the Mind, requiring no physical recording of the information learned from such a mental process.

(M) Alchemy- a magical power capable of changing an object from its natural base to become different in nature from its original base was.

(N) Cosmo – The Universe functioning as a systematic arranged whole, operating in Harmony, Order, and Balance, causing it to be a Divine system, caused by the Divine Essence.

(O) Inertia – A state of resistance to motion and change, yet is able to produce elements to be in form, motion and change.

To appear as if not there, but is there.

(P) Solvent – A liquid that can dissolve another liquid

The Divine Essence (God)

Chapter 1

I will begin with the way I will end this book and that is being Divinely Truthful with you, desiring what I write will serve as an inspiration to all who find the interest and courage to read it.

It is not necessary that you agree with what I am sharing with you, because that is not my motivation for writing this book.

I do not take into thought what your opinion will be concerning what I write about in this book, I just give to you in writing what has been revealed to me about a multiple of topics that is common to the interest and belief of the world.

I am confident with that which I share with you, knowing it will be something new and Different from what you already been told to believe about the topics I will write about in this book consisting of Divine Spiritual Revelation.

I have chose to write first about the most talked about and to most, the most complex entity in and out of this world of the two universe, one ethereal and the other materially physical.

Within the two universes, there remain the same energy Action that is the cause for all we are able to look at and all we must be able to see.

There are occurrences that happen beyond our sense of perception and by the action of our mind; we are capable of looking at all things physical and seeing not all that are physical.

Such an action performed because of the Oneness of the Divine Essence, the Divine energy that is without visible material.

Yet it is a Substance without form or appearance, real or symbolic, its intelligence is verified by the way the Energy of Darkness reveal the Glow of the Physical Universe.

The Energy Of Darkness and all that happen to be and not to be verify the forever presence of the Divine Essence that act without Motive.

The Fool it is who attempt to define the Divine Essence and the Fool it is who know not the Divine essence.

We all search for the level within us that will put us in contact with our Divine Spirituality, a feat that cannot be accomplished without the knowledge of thyself.

All things physical there dwell within is the Divine Essence, that which is of the Divine Spatial Darkness, verifying the Dimension of Eternity and Infinity, leaving no room to speculate or to be believed, during the course of your body life experience.

Many have an inability to See and Know about that which the Divine Essence has produced and it is the Divine Essence that give to us our role to play in the Court house of the Physical Universe, in which our Life role is acted out to the finish of our Lives journey on this earth.

If you do not know from whence you come, then how do you know to where you go and without knowledge about such a journey, then how do you justify your life for being what you know not of it to be?

Because you do not know the Divine Dimension of the Divine Essence, with the proof of your Divine Spirituality being with the knowledge that there is no proof to be known of the Divine Essence, and it is that Wisdom that indicate the Infinite Intelligence of the Divine Essence, the God of Now and Then, and Never More.

Such knowledge verifies the Divine Essence, which is beyond our conventional ability to know of that which we have an inability to know about.

So to be able to comprehend what has just been revealed to you concerning the Divine Essence, such a comprehension is what gives you the ability to desire to experience your Divine Spirituality.

You must be able to elevate into the domain of the Divine Ethereal World of Eternal Infinity, where Body, Mind, and Conscious can not go, there is a requirement for you to know of the Divine Essence and what it is not.

We have a saying that two things we do not debate, which is God and Religion, yet those are the two that require a belief of that which have the world under control today.

When you think about the two, they are really one and the same, though their role may be different.

So I will concentrate on the God role, which is a role played created by Man, he using the title God and it is the relationship that God and religion has that has been developed to be the same.

Religion has the world in a state of belief concerning God, while you are to believe that God is the Spirit of religion.

Therefore, you cannot discuss one without exposing the other and each espouses to be related one to the other.

It is depended on how we believe about each of them that give to them meaning, so it is within a religious context that God take on the persona of religion. God is upon a religious foundation.

 God is religious and is based upon man ideals about God and God has been presented by Man to represent a belief system that is of a required mental action of faith, and hope.

 Now the question is, where is the spirituality in a setting where God is of the persona of Man and religion is depended upon the belief of Man, so based upon these set of facts, can we assume with a conclusion that God and Religion is of the Mind of Man ?

I have presented this set of facts concerning God and Religion, so now I can clearly insinuate to you that the Divine Essence in a Spiritual act of acknowledgement is entirely different in action without meaning or description.

A God with meaning and a purpose, with a description, such a God is man creation but the Divine Essence, being the ethereal Nature of all things that it is, while the God of religious being of the Nature of Man.

So when desiring to reach the deeper higher ethereal Divine Spiritual action that is of and within your life self, it require for you to know what the Divine Essence does not constitute as oppose to what the God of religion constitute, with the Divine Essence being the essential to Everything that is and it is not.

The God of religion is of everything which man has played a part in creating " He " has created a religion of profane belief and not a theology that you are required to know.

It is essential to your Divine Spirituality that you know and understand the difference between the Divine Essence and the God of religion, the Divine Essence is the "God" of existence, the eternal infinite DARK space with no beginning or ending.

In existence is where only the Divine Truth and Reality reside, they being the principles of the Divine Essence, and by its Divine Inert presence, it cause the physical universe to be and it is the physical universe that cause life to become its physical reality.

 The religious God become the God of life yet in all things that is and will come to be, it is the Divine Essence that is essential to all things to be, and there is none that exceed the absolute of the Divine Essence, the presence that has no beginning nor an Ending to all it does and all it reveal to be.

The physical universe gets its life by the mere presence of the Divine Essence and it is the God of religion that assign principles of qualification to life in the physical universe.

Man the Human Being is the creator of the Religious God of Life, coming with instruction of engagement and with a perception of there being a beginning and ending to the process of life, it being a physical body in action.

The Divine Essence is the essential inert ethereal action of intelligence, which is eternally infinite existence and by its existence, all else become the physical life (motion) of its action, a nonphysical and physical motion of continuous coming and going, from existence to life, and from life to existence, never the twain to be in the company of the same dimension, separate from each in its action.

Life is for the physical body and existence is the inert ethereal eternal infinite Intelligent Energy, having no beginning or ending, alternating not between dimensions, but the Divine Essence is essential to all life dimensional action and is eternal existence.

In our life of religious belief we have been told to believe that God is an intelligent Being that has emotion with desire and expectation about all that "He" has created and that God is in physical form with a Mind that reason and make decision for corporeal life form, but it is the nonreligious God, the Divine Essence, that produce and reveal all there is To Be and do so without motive or precondition for the way all that It has revealed is to actual behave in the physical life form It has produced.

So it is the God of Divine Essence that produce Life in a form that has the intelligent mind to reason, giving it the freedom with what we call having the freedom of will and is with the ability to make choices, without the influence of the Divine Essence, the God of and is in everything It has produced,

Yet it is intelligent life form, developed to express itself with the mind that guide that life form and is with a spirit that is displayed either Divinely or profanely.

It is only with the Divine Mind that you are capable of going into the ethereal world of existence and the knowledge and understanding gained from such a journey, is what cause your life in the physical dimension to be a Divine Spiritual Life.

So, life is about knowing and understanding, and it is the Divine Mind of intelligence that give life living ability to make decisions that will be Divine.

Also, life without the use of its Divine Mind end up being with a profane Mind, a quality of mind that provide you with information that will cause you to make decisions that are not of a Divine intelligent mind.

It is such a profane Mind action that can cause your life living to become full of misery and painfully depressing, a life condition that the God of Divine Essence play no part in causing in your life living experiences and does not issue out any warning or threats to your body Life.

The Divine Essence is the actuality of eternity and infinity, it being the reason and cause for everything to become in all physical type of forms and with a life mind that is capable of reasoning and making decisions that will determine the quality of life you will live, such a God is without motive or predetermination for your life mind way of living.

Mankind has come to believe that they have the ability to challenge the Divine Essence and can prove that they can mathematically calculate and accurately measure any and everything the Divine essence has produced.

Man by his action make claim that he is equal to God and having the ability to create all things and to be able to mathematically prove it.

When using the method of math in his effort to try and prove that all things can be mathematically measured and can be proved to be the truth and reality of that which math has been used to verify to be the fact of all matter.

Man claim all things can be mathematically proven either to be true or to be real, he claim to be the creator of God.

Man religious God it must be, because that which is cannot become the creator of that which has produced you To Be.

First of all what is math other than a system of symbols created by mankind to use to justify that which mankind believe, but do not know.

That which you do not know, can not be proved to be what you believe it to be. The fact that mankind is, prove that mankind is not self created; it is the Divine Essence of the Energy that can not be mathematically calculated.

It is the darkness out of which mankind and all other life forms have come, mankind coming with the concept of math, a concept which mankind has created and now use to measure for reason to make claim to believe about what is Divinely Real and True.

Yet, the fact is, what we refer to as truth and real, such being the principals that can not be mathematically proved, because it is the Divine Essence that is the inert, ethereal and infinite embodiment of Divine Truth and Reality.

So the Divine Essence cannot be figured out, much about that Infinite deity just must be acknowledged and Its Existence to be verified by the fact that mankind make claim that math can prove everything that is To Be Or Not To Be.

Yet math method is utilized because of the fact of the Divine Essence is the reason for the method used for verification of that which mankind believe to be made to be the facts about all things, using the concept of math, it being the method of undisputable verification.

It is mankind who do not know that which provide mankind with the ability to make such claims about what mankind believe to be the truth of the matter that is being mathematically calculated.

Infinity is out of bound of math calculation; the Divine Essence is Eternally Infinite!

Yet Such a Divine Essence (God) is not the authority of confusion, but is the Divine essence that provides you with the freedom of mind ability to make decisions for your life way to live its life.

Your body life is the minds that reveal your Divine Spirituality, which is what reveal to you, all that is, and Is Not.

The Divine Essence needs not math to verify the Divine truth and Reality of Its Divine Existence.

Universe:

Chapter 2

In order to understand your spirituality you must have a sense of knowledge about the UNIVERSE, all three of them, the inner universe of your self, the physical universe consisting of objects, stars, planets and the ethereal elements, and there is the nonphysical universe, which is the Eternal Infinite spatial Darkness, where therein and thereof, reside the Divine Essence, the not physical entity, God.

I have had the experience of taking a nonphysical journey into the universe, not to have had it to happen from premeditative preparation it just happen, not in the conventional meditation form of a ritual.

As for as I know, it just happen, and it did while I was in the spirit of thought writing a book title Lies About God, not a book that will require much of your Time to finish reading if ever engaged to do so.

There I was in a Dimension that I was made fully aware of and was given to see the Physical Universe in which one of my foot rest and the other, came to rest in the nonphysical spatial Darkness, as if I was set in the physical and the nonphysical.

Behold I heard a voice coming from the Eternal Infinite Space of Darkness, instructing me to look and see to learn and I beheld the physical Universe in a counter clock wise motion.

The objects of the physical universe motion was clock wise and I saw the Mass of gases giving the physical universe a floor like appearance and throughout that Mass I saw many cavities, which I immediately called out to be Black holes.

Not verbally did I yell out but mentally, and it was as if there were entities ingrained in the power of the Infinite Darkness, because it seem as if to be reading my mind thoughts.

A voice came from the darkness as I could see the Energy waves intrinsic therein but emanating out from the Divine Darkness informing me that there is no such a phenomena as Black Holes.

Such an appearance of such an anomaly in the universe can and does occur and do occur, because of the power of the universe action.

So there occurred before my mind the appearance of Black holes in the Gas Mass of the universe and such cavities can cause the assumption of there being Black holes throughout the physical Universe.

The truth is that the spatial Darkness Universe is without holes in it and it is without Black Holes.

Darkness is the Black mass of infinity that cannot be penetrated, there is no holes in the cover of the Divine Infinite Darkness, the infinite Universe.

So, there only could be the appearance of Black holes occurring in the mass of the physical universe.

The universe is important when trying to understand your inner self and such an effort require for you to mental extend into the Metaphysical ethereal Dimensional of thyself.

The mind being the pathway that leads you to the outer Dimensions that is beyond the nature of the First Principle of your physical body Life, it being the body self of you and the inner self-being the universe.

It is important to master the knowledge of such an inner Divine entity, self in motion, because it symbolize and represent an inner action of your ethereal self and can enable you to express your Divine Spirituality.

Your Divine Spirituality is a part of you that require you to be in Harmony with your inner self, as the Universe Spirit harmonizes with your inner self.

Doing so in a Vibration action, expressing a Harmonic behavior, which resonate throughout the Eternal space time, which verify the binary relationship between all things that is a part of the physical Universe.

The Universe is the badge of the Divine Essence and contrary to what is believed about the Universe appearing to have a beginning; such is not what I was told about the universe.

The Universe has neither beginning nor an ending it is liken unto the Soul of all Beings and we will learn that both actions is generated by the Energy of the Divine Essence.

The Divine Essence has no beginning or ending and what the Divine Essence has produced, such has no beginning or ending, it all is a part of a perpetual continuum.

So when dealing with the Universe, we are dealing with an action process that is forever coming and going, an action process that can not be pin pointed as to having a beginning or ending,.

Everything is just a continue Change from being not physical to being physical to not physical again, so it is with the action of the Soul, mind, Spirit continuum, operating in the body life is what give meaning to life and death.

The Universe is not a dead immutable entity, the Universe is alive, its proof of Life is its forever continue motion and by its Motion it send out Vibrating Harmonics that resonate Sounds that are full of Energy, generating a Divine expression that is indicating the presence of a Divine Intelligence.

The Divine Essence is Intrinsically is the institutive soul of the Divine Darkness and therein is the Divine Essence, (God) the entity that is beyond defining.

Yet ITS Proof of being Divinely True and Real Is the Eternal Infinite Dark Spatial Universe, out of which come the presence of the physical Universe, the spatial universe being the sacred perfect Infinite Darkness whose Night should be embraced and not feared.

There within the perfect night reside Divine information about all things concerning and is of the universe life, with the Darkness serving as the cover for the Divine Essence, IT being the Producer of everything there is , ever was, and ever will be, even that which is constituting the presence of the physical Universe.

So when dealing with the physical universe you are observing the objects thereof, it consisting of all objects whose life is of the universe elements, which is the nature of all things, above and beyond, where life is limited and the soul existence is forever present.

It is the Spirituality of the Universe that has its effect upon its inner and outer action, affecting the various compositions of its bodies.

So the Body Life, consisting of the elements in cellular form, having the ability of sense and mind, each responding to the spiritual harmonics of the universe, being generated from the action of the cellular elements of life.

The Body Life has a unique ability to perform referring to such a performance as being Life in motion action, having the sensibility to detect as well as the mental ability to reflect about that which Life detect.

Life is the sense of response and the mind of reason making you to be aware of and to know life physical and thoughtful experiences.

Now, what does all of this mean, it mean that the Universe as well, is alive with intelligence and it does consist of Cells throughout its Eternal Infinite Existence and Life, one not physical and the other is physical.

Existence is referring to the Universe of Darkness and Life refers to the Universe that consists of objects in the physical, they that form the physical universe.

It is the physical universe that is receiving its energy which is emanating from the Spatial Darkness is what cause life to be of the physical universe.

The Divine Essence causes the Body life to have a Sense to Mind relationship, generated by the Divine energy that is operating in the body life, which cause life expression in various and different ways.

The Divine Energy is a part of the physical life and Metaphysic existence, with the physical being that of life sense-mind conscious experience and the Metaphysical being that of the existing Mind-Spiritual Intuitive action that is occurring beyond the conscious and subconscious level.

In the elemental make up of life, it is the Mind Energy of Life that has the connection and relationship with the universal bodies, each bonded to each other and is coming from the Eternal Infinite Energy of the Divine Essence.

The Space Darkness is the Greater Good beyond all things and the Divine Ethereal Energy, it being the Divine Intelligence of the Divine Essence, (God) serving to be the Mind enclosed within the Eternal Infinite Space Darkness.

You have been taught to fear and disrespect, the Universal Infinite spatial Darkness yet it serve to be the Spirituality of Space and Motion and Life and Time, all is One and is Of The Divine Essence.

So all things are a part of the physical Universe that is physical and all things not being physical, is of the spatial Universe, it being the Mind Intelligence of Life and Existence.

Therefore, it is the physical universe that interacts with your Life Spirituality, as well as with your Mind Spirituality, the two being one in the action of expression.

One level being of Sense-Mind action, it being physical and on the metaphysical level that level is beyond the physical level and is the Dimension of the nonphysical, it being out of conscious into the Ethereal Existence where there is Divine Spiritual Truth and Reality coexisting on the realm where the Divine intelligence is that of the Divine Essence.

So our sense-mind spirituality has to do with our life active reflection of our attitudinal behavior on the physical level and on such a level is the expression of our life spirit.

The spirit indicate the way we act and react to events that take place in the universe that is affecting our life Sense-mind that cause an expressed attitudinal behavior, revealing the quality of your life sense-mind interactive ability to reason rationally and logically, or irrational and illogical.

Behavioral attitude is a reflection of the quality of your life spirituality, be it of a sense-mind expression or a Mind –thought expressed action, the formal being a spirituality expressed on the Life profane physical level and the latter being a Spirit expressed on Life Divine Mind-Thought Dimension, each revealing an attitude and behavior that is associated to your Life through mind expression, one physical and the other ethereal nonphysical.

To know the universe you must understand its function and the effectiveness it has in affecting the mind of all life because the universe action is what cause all life Beings Mind to be able to be self expressive.

The universe has nothing to do with the quality of your mind but with you having the ability to express your mind, which provides you with the ability to display a quality of spirit that is reflective of your mind activity.

 So whether or not the spirit being displayed is A Divine expression or a profane expression, it reveals the quality of your spirituality.

The universe is a gigantic organism, sitting upon the lap of the Eternal Infinite spatial Dark Universe, it is the forever night that produces light and all of the elements needed for life to be in all forms and all life is of the universe organism.

There are myriads of cells that make up the universe there among them is one of those cells residing our Milky Way Galaxy and in there you will find our Solar System consisting of what is referred as planets revolving around a Star and one of those planets revolving around the Star – Sun, is the planet we refer to as Earth.

The earth it is where we reside, there within one of those cells of the physical universe and within every one of those cells, there is Divine intelligent existing Energy.

We use the Divine Energy to perform in life spirit reflect the behavior of that life that can be different due to our life phenotype when we are in our own physical presence in the universal cell.

Life Nature consist of Soul, Body, Mind and Spirit in physical form with a Metaphysical Ethereal presence of existence being in the nature of a dual Being, one in physical form and the other inertly ethereal without form within the Body Life.

The physical gigantic living cell which we call the universe, consist of One Divine Energy that is provided by the forever Divine Space Darkness, which its Divine Energy is present, in all of its universal cellular structure.

It is that Energy that equip us with the ability to be physical and Ethereal, we being able to express a Spirituality that come from the Mind and is expressed physically as well as ethereal, each occurring on a different level of our Life Mind function.

There is a requirement of you, in order to experience a Divine Spiritual Life way of living, you have to be able to make the connection with the Divine Energy Intelligence, that which is of our Universe Cellular structure, it is within that cellular structure a Cell in which our Solar

System reside and it is your mind that is in connection with the Divine Energy residing within your body life.

People are told to attempt to make contact with our Cellular Divine Energy, referring to it as being our God, that which must be reached by the use and act of Prayer, which I intend to get more into later on in this book.

So to give you an idea of the Divine Spirituality that is experienced in life and the fact that your spirit reveal the Being that you are, such require a universe mental connection which require an awareness by you about the universe.

So to get to know the meaning and purpose of life, it require for you to know and understand the meaning and purpose of both universe, one Ethereal and the other is physical, with the latter being the Child of the Former, the former being the Ethereal Infinite Spatial Darkness, which you are told to believe represent Evil.

There is enough information concerning the Universe until there can be written myriads of volumes of books about it, so I am just giving you only a small fraction of information about the Universe in order to prep you about what is to come in this book about your Divine Spirituality and how your Life can gain benefit from knowing about such an intimate part of your Life Being, and the universe is just that.

There is nothing that measure up to express its spirituality than the universe and in such a Divine fashion, the universe express and demonstrate how we the people should live our lives, as It, in its Divine motion, sing Divine melodies that come from its Harmonic resonant motion sending out to us electromagnetic vibration, which are all a part of that magnificent universal action that is putting us in a spirit that is generated by the soul and is expressed by our Mind action, which is demonstrated by our body life spirit. (Attitude and behavior)

The physical Universe being of such magnification, displaying such a Divine spirit in its action and by it being the offspring of the Eternal Infinite Universe, the Physical Universe could not have had a beginning and most certainly don't have a End Time, because as one part leave, there come another to maintain the consistency of the physical universe.

Parts of the physical universe come and go individually but collectively the body of the universe remains in harmony with the Infinite Universe.

So there is no measuring of Time that is of such continued infinite universe action, meaning, what Eternity and Infinity has produced, such being the spatial darkness which is the infinite universe, that which has produced the physical universe, causing it not to have had a beginning nor to have an ending, which Time can not accurately measure.

Because the Physical Universe is the Spirit of the not physical Universe, which is the Eternal Infinite Spatial Darkness, each having not a beginning or an Ending, such is the character of your Life Soul, which cause you to be able to express and demonstrate your Life Spirituality as well as your Self Spirituality, which is looked at and seen by your Sense of Mind, the Physical and Spirit of your Life Mind Body action.

The physical Universe is a profound organ caused by infinite Intelligence and it is the physical universe that express its spirit in such a way to verify and validate that there is a more profound Soul that is the cause of the Physical Universe and you being a part of the physical universe.

So when in an attempt to connect with your infinite Spirituality, which is a action done by your Mind Self, your Mind must be able to interface and interact with the Divine Eternal Infinite Universe, the Divine Essence to and of us all.

Such an act can put you in actual experience with your Divine Spiritual Self, which will enable you to travel into vast and various Dimensions of your self, which give you the ability to learn and to know with understanding, about all that has been of question by you, concerning the Divine Essence, (God) the Universe, and your Life Being.

The Key to knowing and Understanding the Mysteries of Life, revealed by your mind and is expressed by your Divine Spirituality, is your Soul, and it is your Mind Lock, which your Soul unlocks, that allow you to enter the doorway into the alchemy (Magic) corridors of the

Divine Sacred Holy Darkness, the sacred darkness being the Garment that cover the Divine Essence. (God)

I know how extensive and dramatic your belief has been conditioned to be against the Mass of Darkness, having you to associate all things that is the opposite to what you have been conditioned to associate with to be the Greater Good and to label such an opposite to that Greater Good life experience as being that of Darkness, which represent to you, "Evil ."

You have been taught to believe Darkness represent the unaccepted and unpleasant side of life experience, meaning the "Bad"side of what we associate to be the Greater Good which only come out from the light as you are told, you not knowing that Divinity and Darkness coalesce with each other and is the epitome of the holiness of the Divine Essence and the light is substandard when it come to the Divine Darkness.

So in Divinity there is no need for classification of the standard of life expression, all under such a Divine presence is in Harmony, Order, and Balance, in all its does.

So, when ever you mischaracterize the Divine Mass Darkness, it being the essential Cloak of the Divine Essence, resting on the Throne of Eternal Infinity, you disavow of having any knowledge with Understanding of the divine Essence (God) and it is that Ignorance that will prevent you from experiencing your Divine Spirituality, which has direct relationship to both

Universe, the Ethereal and the Physical, the Two being One Of Each Other.

I know what I am sharing with you in this book is counter productive to what you have been taught concerning the entity Darkness and how it effect life and is responsible for our Body Life.

It is in these Times that the Divine Truth has come to you, a Time of Revealed Enlightenment and not everybody will be mentally qualified to accept the Divine Truth, as I am now revealing it to you.

So you ask the question, why should you believe me, my response to your question is that you should not believe me, but you should come to know you, and with such knowledge with understanding, you will come to know of that which this book is now revealing to you about your Divine Spirituality.

Spirituality transcend your Religious Spirituality, the one that teach you to disavow any respect for the Massive Eternal Infinite Universal Darkness, it being the Key to you reaching and understanding your Divine Spirituality, which I will reveal more in depth to you later on in this book.

the profound universe is that shade of space that is without light, it is what we have come to label as being dark, black, we call it night, and such a shade we have come to describe to be the source of evil, bad luck, gruesomely depressing, the symbol of death, and is the opposite of all we have learned to associate with light.

Light is what we accept to be perfectly good, we have even assigned light to be superior over Darkness and as long as we subscribe to such a belief being true, then we will not be able to experience our Divine Spirituality.

Because being in the expression of your spirituality will cause such an ascension into the dimension of the metaphysical and at such a Divine level you will know the mystery that awaits you within that universal curtain we call Night, darkness, which is the source of all of our Light.

The infinite Universe is the Darkness we call night, it is the Mother of Existence and the Father of Life and within the Dark bosom of Existence, its Divine chalice, there reside all of the Elements necessary for all things to become as they appear to be in physical form.

There are the elements without form, they being ingredients also of the universe which is capable and qualified to produce and sustain life and such knowledge about that Dark Universe must be divinely known.

Such is a requirement of you, that is if we are to travel into the ethereal domain of our intuitive self, the domain where conscious mind is not required nor is allowed in order to know what need to be known about all that mystify you about all you are incapable of looking at but desire to see.

The Divine universe is a phenomena with and without its physical parts that are visible and its elements that are not visible, both universe is worthy to be praise, the universe being the immediate attribute that signify and verify that there is a Divine Intelligent Essence which cause motion to be, and not to be, it is that which is without and is within both of the Universe.

Religion

Chapter 3

Now, let us turn our attention to religion and its approach to Spirituality, I must inform you that Divine Spirituality which this book is about, and it is not about religion, it is about a Divine Quality Of Life that put your life in a living state of Harmony, Order, and Balance when in the process of Divine Thinking, which your Life is entitle to.

So since religion is about threatening your Life, make it kind of difficult for it to bring peace to your life, which is what Divine Thinking will do, it produce a Spirituality that will become common to your body life and such Divine Thinking is meant to do for your Life what religion can't do for your body life.

This book is not meant to be a put down on religion and all who are comfortable in your religion, that is what is of value to you, but I do make a distinction between Religion and Divine Spirituality, which require an entirely different approach to the Theology of Life, as it relate to the Divine Essence.

Religion and Divine Spirituality travel two different paths in your Mind, so in this chapter I will deal primarily with religion to show how it could impede your Divine Spirituality instead of enhancing it, intentional or not, something Divine Spirituality will not do.

What is religion other than a cultist institution with a doctrine to guide and instruct you in how you are to behave in life and if obedient to its doctrine, it tell you what to expect in another life after this one.

Religion is a mean of controlling your mind thoughts about things that come to be a part of your body life, it is that which feed you and condition you to become fearful of its God and to eschew the Darkness, the Sacred Domain of the Divine Essence, (God) that which does not instruct nor threaten you, nor make promise nor make Commands of you, which religion does to your life.

You can not come to discover your Divine Spirituality under the cloak of Fear, it must come to be no longer a part of your life involvement and you must come to treat Self as a part of life to be not worthy of suffering in order to please and to get close to the God of Religion.

Religion imply that your Spirit is a separate part of your life and in order for you to enter your Spirit world, you must learn to have your Life to suffer long and be piteously, in order to please your religious God, such an act does not show an act of appreciation to the Divine Gift of Life, which is worthy of experiencing a Spirituality of Peace and Joy in Life.

There are two types of Spirituality, one is Divine and the other is Profanely religious and it is Religion Spirituality that render to you a life belief that is full of lies and deceit, which is the Spirit of Fear and false promises, and it is religion that represent a Doctrine that Deceive you and point you away from your self, such an act is an evil projection of a Spirit, all being done in the name of religion.

We have entered the dispensation of Time which bring to your Life an enlightenment about the Divine need for your self and it is this Time that call for a reawakening of you and to have you to participate in your Life pursuit of its goals, which will bring, not fear but bravery, not weakness but strength, and not self sacrificing, but self elevation and protection, such an action take you through the door way into Divine Spirituality and not Religious Spirituality.

So many Lies and acts of Deception has been presented to you about your Life, done in the name of religion, a religion that teach you to look away from your self and not into your self.

So a religion that point you away from your self is a religion that is more about fear and death than is about bravery and Life, such a religious spirit does not bode well with Life but is out to destroy your Life by misguiding your life.

In religion, you are always looking to go physically some where with God and to God, such be the Spirituality of Religion, never to get you to See the depth inside of your self and how far it extend into your self Dimension that extend into Infinity, it being a Spirituality that express the Wisdom of knowing, understanding, and experiencing the intimacy of your ethereal self.

In religion, life is more profanely physical Spiritual, than is Divinely Spiritual, religion has more to do with your physical expressed Spirit of believing, more so than with your Spiritual expression of knowing about your inner self.

Divine spirituality put you on a mental course of a revealed experiences with the Universe, your past lives experiences, and your life Present experiences, concerning the two selves, they being of your physical Life and your Ethereal Self Existence.

Life is only pertaining to the physical, past and present, while Existence is pertaining to the Ethereal aspect of your self, which exceed your life self experiences, where past and present become the all of your physical life experiences, playing no part in the state of existence, there where Time is of no measure of past and present.

Life has nothing to do with a future involvement, which is a speculation about life to be in a period of time not yet come, so only Divine Truth and Reality should be of your concern about determining the things that your life is to be involved with and it being the Past and Present of which our lives should be concerned with in living our lives, something religion will not teach you.

The Now and Then of our lives experiences, is the degree of Time in which your Life Revolve in the physical, because in the ethereal Spiritual action of your Mind Self, Time does not reside in the realm of existence, only Eternity and Infinity is existence companion.

A Life Being, is not a part of Ethereal Existence and existence is not a part of a Life Being, a life Being, is the physical and Existence is the Ethereal nonphysical revealing the Spirit of your Mind action, which verify Divine Truth and Reality throughout the Universe, with the Divine Truth being not the basis for all religious belief about God, Universe, and the Physical Self.

Religion have you to be in pursuit of a God you are not certain about, its main theme is to have you to believe in the God " Him " and to have you to have faith in "Him" and to have hope that what you believe about "Him" (God) will be of benefit to you in a life to come.

Religion promise you a life in a place and Time to come that will preserve your life for ever, such a belief is performed by people who are organized into a gathering religious cults.

It is religion that require such a belief in heaven, to the point that such a life pursuit is all about what you must do for God and what God will do for your life and not what you are obligated to do for your life now, right here in this Time for your life enjoyment on this planet.

Yet, it is a religious belief that have you in a religious spirituality that is about pleasing God and not your Life today, and it is being under such a religious indoctrination that have you in such a pursuit of everlasting life and not a divine sustainable life on this earth.

Therefore, you being in such a religious spirituality, is why the world is in the condition it is in today, which is not a world of love and compassion for THE LIFE OF ALL BEINGS, but a life of individual competition for the things of the world, which has caused evil to be a part of your spiritual expression.

Religion throws you off of your self center by having you to be in pursuit of its God and not of the knowledge of the self of your life, yet it is your life which God has provided you with, which seem to me should have us to be with a desire to do the things that will please our life and not harm our life.

We must do the things in our lives that will protect our lives and in doing so, it would put us in a state to compliment our lives instead of being in pursuit to save our lives by confessing to believe in a man made religion which indicate that our lives are in a constant state of trouble.

In religion it teaches you to believe that your obligation is to please God which does seem to set well with the religious God, when your concern should be about pleasing ourselves and not the Divine Essence. (God)

Even though it is the Divine Essence that is the cause for our life to be, the Divine Essence does not solicit anything from that which It has caused to be.

The objective in life is to please ourselves and not God, because it is God that is not in need of pleasure, only your life is, and to please life is to respect all life and such an act is the display of Divine Spirituality and not religious spirituality, which have you involve with pleasing God and not the self of all life, which is what Divine Spirituality is all about in life, wherever it is in this physical universe.

It is religious spirituality that have you seeking the Light in which the presence of the religious God is claimed to reside, according to the teaching of religion, which require for you to have a belief, faith, and hope.

Religion make claim that God is within the light and that he is the Light of the world and not in and above the world, it is such a religious beliefs that prevent you from knowing what is beyond the conscious Mind of your Life Self and it is that prevention that keep you from elevating beyond the conscious Mind into the realm of your Divine intuitive Ethereal Spiritual Self.

Such an elevation out of the conscious Mind is that which only Divine Spirituality is qualified to take you into such a Dimension that is beyond Mind activity, and that is where the Divine Essence of Divine Truth and Reality reside, needing not the crutches of belief, faith, and hope to spawn such a false Truth and Reality about a religious God.

There is a Truth and Reality which is centered around pleasing God and saving your Life and not about pleasing self and enjoying Life in this world.

It is religion that has given to you a God that is believed to have come to make commands of you, claiming there is a son of the religious God, while it is the Sun-Star that is in and beyond the world that verify that it is the Sun of The Perfect Night, which is intrinsic within the Divine Darkness and it is the Divine Essence that cause all things To Be..

This book is about Divine Beings Spirituality and is not about Human Beings religious Spirituality, this book is meant to reveal to you the ability of the Soul – Mind being capable of elevating you into the realm of a dimension where Mind thought is not required to believe concerning the Divine Truth and Reality about the Divine Essence and both Universe.

It is beyond the Mind Life activity that out from the domain of such action there is the Eternal Dark Infinite Space, the residence of the Divine Essence, (GOD) where eternal Divine inert ethereal action constantly without ceasing does occur.

So life endeavor should be to enter not into the illusion of light but to enter the Divine Reality of the Eternal Infinite Darkness, because there is where the Divine Spirit action of the Divine Essence reside and only in the action of your Divine Spirituality, you will get to know about such a profound Truth about all that mystify you about that you are capable of looking at using the sense of your body mind.

To know about all things that concern you, then you must be capable of seeing all that is not capable of being looked at on the surface of your sense Mind life action, such is why the need to enter into your Divine Spirituality and not a religious spirituality, the Divine Spirituality is required of your Divine Mind.

Even though there are many references to Spirituality within a religious context and there are many claims that suggest rituals to be used to help you get into the so call Spiritual world dimensions.

I do not subscribe to such allegation concerning what is referred to as Religious Spirituality, which is measured by your believing commitment to a religious doctrine that weigh your life worth by the belief, faith, and hope, that you have in a religious doctrine.

It is the gravity of your religious beliefs that determines and measures your Spirituality and it seemed to be implied that there is a Spirit entity that is separate from your physical Self spirit, that kind of belief have much to say about your spirituality in religion.

Religion carries a very huge following of believers and this is in no way to be taken as an attack upon religion, more so than a revelation of the Divine Truth about religious Spirituality.

Divine Spirituality is represented in the nature as it should be, as it relate to our Lives being in the nature that the Universe has presented us to be, which is a Being not in need of a religious spiritual belief, but is in need of knowledge about our Divine Spiritual Self, which is revealed in the way that we express ourselves toward each other in the world.

I will hold off from defining Spirituality until later, because at this moment, it is our religious character that needs to be defined and classified, because the topic is Spirituality, and it is approached in a Religious context.

Religion is what prevent you from getting to know about the full volume of your Spirituality, a Spirituality if not Divine, has a flaw, and anything with a flaw is not of Divine significance to you, because nothing exceed your Divinity and to reduce it to mean and be something of a religious belief is not to serve you in your Life best interest.

When dealing with Divine Spirituality this Chapter on Religion could not have been avoided, that is if this is to be a book that takes an entirely different knowledgeable approach to present to you for your examination.

This is a book that Demand for you to Think and take no thought about sparing your Religious belief when dealing with a Divine Substance that is important to your Life way of Living, that is if you are serious about learning and getting to know about yourself and your Life Spirituality, Divine it must be to your Life and not religious.

As you should be able to see, I am keeping the information I am sharing with you in this book very simple, it is not my intention to try to impress you by using the familiar so call Spiritual terms to describe your Life Self and your Life spirituality.

It is done often, using metaphysical terms when speaking about spirituality, so I will not do so when dealing with the Truthfulness of yourself, because it is all about your Divine Self when dealing with your Spirituality and not about your religious Physical sensual Self alone.

 Life is about the Body Living, and Divine Spirituality is about the Mind Self existence, the body Life being mostly guided by the body senses and the Mind Self being guided by a Thoughtful and Understanding mental action of the Soul - Mind interaction.

It is the sense to Mind that produce the attitudinal behavioral expression that reveal the quality of yourself Divine Spirituality, it having nothing to do with your religious belief, it is your religious belief that can hinder you from experiencing your Expressed Divine Spirituality, which emanate explicitly from the Sense-Mind interaction.

The Sense to Mind is an indication that the senses are what enable your body to be able to experience a visual perception, a feeling of being touched, an ability to smell aroma, to hear sound, and to taste various flavors, but not before the mind has given the body the ability to experience the evidence of the body senses.

Everything takes effect in the Mind, which is a process of thinking, most Time reduced to believe.

The world in general has been made to be over whelm by the different doctrine of religion, so this is not a book that follow along such a religious path, a path that have you to believe that God is a Being, and is a Male gender.

 Belief will have you to become involved with an interest in saving your Life by having a religious belief about God, believing that religion will take you on a trip into heaven, rather than to have you doing what is required of you with your life, which is to enjoy your Life and protect your life.

 You have the natural ability to choose to live your life while on this earthly realm which involve your body – sense-mind interaction, in a Divine Spiritual way of living, which require living your life in Harmony, Order, And Balance when Thinking.

So as I have said, Life is for the Body and to experience the Mind action that will put yourself into a Spiritual Life of Divine acquaintance, you must learn the difference in living your Life in a Religious spiritual setting or you striving to enter into a Mind awareness that will put you into a Divine Spiritual experience for your life now, the choice is left up to you the reader.

So since this is not a religious book but is a book that is meant to give you an experience to See inside of yourself as oppose to looking away from yourself, it become a decision you the reader must make about your religious choice for your life, or to seek the Divine spiritual way you will live your life.

This book is not meant to denigrate or to elevate religion, it is meant to assist you in acknowledging your Divine Spirituality, an act of life that has nothing to do with religious belief about God but is to help you to get to know about the Divine Infinite Energy Essence. (God)

Fear

Chapter 4

In a world where evil is abound, fear is always present and we ask ourselves why is it that there is so much discord in the world among people today, while some of us blame the world present spirit that it express toward each other as being based upon the ethnic difference of people that constitute the world.

I share with you that it is basically based upon the fear we have of each other as our ethnicity become more different than the others in their separate ethnic groups, all because we all are lacking the proper foundation that qualify us to be able to erase all of our fears from being a part of our Life living experiences.

The proper foundation we are in need of to not allow fear to become a part of our emotional expression, is to know that we must Think our way through Life and not to attempt to believe our way through life and such a Mind method we are lacking, which is what prevent us from living a Divine Spiritual life today.

Fear come from an anticipated result of physical harm that can come from having the lack of knowledge about that which is causing the anxiety that cause you to anticipate harmful results during the process of living.

Fear in life come from a physical experience and it is that Mental posture that will cause you not to be able to express a spirituality that will demonstrate that you are living a life that is in harmony, order, and balance, the required mental posture in order for you to experience a life of Divine Spirituality.

When living a life in fear it cause you to be without confidence in the way you must live your life and where there is no life confidence the spirit of the life you display is full of uncertainty, confusion, and a lack of self confidence.

So without self assurance the spirit can not express a show of peace and joy, emotions that are required if you are to experience Divine Spirituality and not fear.

Fear is what cause you to be off centered with your Mind self and it is the mind that determine the quality of your spirituality, meaning fear has no place within a Divine setting which can only be caused by you knowing thyself, both physical and mentally.

It is being aware of both, your physical and mental self that will serve as evidence that you are the controlling force in determining your Life way of living.

Fear is what interrupt the relationship between the Soul, sense and Mind action and when that Divine Energy is not being received Divinely by your sense and Mind, then the result will be you not being able to enter the ethereal dimension where all of the answers to your Life questions reside.

So it is the quality of your Spirit is what gives you the result of a life that is lived divinely and such a Life living is without Fear.

Fear of that which is not known will cause you to reflect a spirit that is comfortable in only believing about that you do not know and it is such a Life way of living that Evil has the opportunity to become present in your Life Spirituality.

Because you see, Spirituality is not innately Divine or shall I say righteous, it is the Mind that determine your spirit action and the result from that action is what demonstrate the quality of life you are living, because it is your Mind that cause the quality of your Life Spirituality, and it is Fear that is an enemy to your Life ability to live Divinely.

Fear is life interrupter, it is a disease that infect the Mind and whenever the Mind is not at peace in its action, then your Life become infected with viruses that cause a inner action of disharmony, disorder, and an imbalance in the way your physical organs are functioning.

It is that physical condition that can cause what we refer to as death, all because Fear bring about an imbalance in the Mind action and when the Mind is not flowing Divinely, meaning your thoughts, then Life is susceptible to Fear and Fear is an enemy, a disease that prevent Divine Thought.

It is the Mind that determines the quality of your life Spirituality, meaning your attitudinal behavior that you express in your body life daily living.

Fear is not an innate quality of your Mind action, it is the Mind that reveal the nature and quality of your Life living, so no, Life is not meant to be a part of Fear, yet we have allowed Fear to become a part of our Life way of living.

It is that fear which has brought death and destruction into our life way of living and we have learned to accept such a way of living with Fear, as if it is a normal way of living.

So I share with you that anything that interfere with your Divine way of living, is not a normal process of Life, meaning FEAR IS NOT NORMAL TO LIFE !

Fear is only an acquired emotional behavior expressed by your life mental action, so conquer Fear and you will be able to experience the uninterrupted relationship that is of the Soul- Sense to Mind-Body interaction.

Such an action is what causes you to be able to experience an expression reflecting your Divine Spirituality.

It is the Divine Master Teacher that is in the know of the spiritual action of the physical Universe as well as the ethereal universe.

Fear stifle your ability to mentally elevate and whenever there is something that can interfere with your ability to Think in Harmony with your Soul action, then your life become as unstable as your thoughts are.

Without Divine thoughts, meaning thoughts that are reasonable, rational and logically, then it become very difficult if not impossible to experience an expression of your Divine Spirituality, which should be the goal of all Life Intelligence.

You can not become of benefit to your Life if your life is govern by Fear, when it is Fear that arrest the Mind and when the Mind is in captivity, your Life become the prisoner of Fear, causing you to have no interest in delving into the metaphysical levels beyond your Mind action.

It is the metaphysical level where those that are privileged to the esoteric experience, which take place away from your Mind physical exoteric experience concerning yourself activities that allow you to know what is Divinely True and Real concerning the mysteries of the Universe.

Fear only benefit the workers of evil, liars, and deceivers, it has no respectful standing within the Divine Spiritual Mind, it serve as only a hindrance to the ability to reason divinely and fear should be defeated at every approach it take toward your Mind.

Fear is a very devastating foe for the Mind to have in life and should never be allowed to enter into the domain of your Divine Spirituality, because the moment that fear is allowed to be a part of your life, your Divinity weaken and soon come not to be anymore of your Body life way of living in this world.

I am sharing this important fact of information about Fear with you, because I know, with the presence of fear in your life, it will be your life that will be prevented from enjoying the Divinity of your life and it will be fear that will cause you not to explore the deeper level into your Mind intuitive dimension.

So fear being in your mind will cause your life to be unstable, which will cause you not to be able to express your Divine Spirituality which is what keep you grounded in the behavior that keep your Body Life protected from Fear.

If you do not control your mind, and mind is your body life, and it is the control of mind that protect your body life from being exposed to and from expressing the emotion of fear, then it is fear absent in the mind that is required, so that you may enjoy life.

So in order for all of your thoughts about the Divine Essence, (God) both Universe, and Life as a Gift to you, then your thoughts of profound reasoning must be in Harmony, Order, and Balance, concerning those things in and beyond life, those things that you are curious about in life will become clear to you.

Yet, it will be fear that will cause the imbalance of your Mind equilibrium and where there is no harmony of body sense to Mind, then there is no Divinity, and fear become the ruler of your Mind life.

It is a Divine Mind that is required of your life, that is, if you are to express your Divine Spirituality in life, an act of showing temperance in the way that your body life is lived.

Fear is as a devil to the soul, it is always attempting to interrupt the Divine information that is continuously coming from the Soul to the Mind, causing it to be an interlocking action between the Soul-Mind, one causing the other to be, yet it is the Soul that is incapable of being subjected to Fear, only the Mind, when not clothed in its Divinity can experience such weakness and it is weakness that fear feast upon in your life way of living.

So why do we fear, we fear when ever there is something that we are uncertain about, so to be uncertain about your Life and the things that confront your life, make you not to be the master of your life, which give fear the opportunity to become the master of your Life and it is such a life of fear that lives in doubt, which is no more than a state of belief.

A life in fear is always full of misery, such is not the life of a Divine Being, it is the life of the Human Being, they that teach you that it is alright to be fearful in Life, such teaching about fear, serve as a blockade of the path that lead you to your Divine Spirituality.

Divine Spirituality is a quality of Mind capable of taking you into the abyss of the Sacred Eternal Infinite Darkness, the perfect Night, and the Infinite Universe where the Divine Essence is in constant and continue action.

It is Divinity which cause the Divine energy to be the Eternal Infinite Intelligence which is the producer and verifier of all things that Is and Is Not, and is caused by the divine intelligence which has no beginning or ending.

You can not get to know the Divine Essence in the presence of fear, one is immune from the other and the emotion fear, it impede your knowledge about that which you need to know about, concerning the Divine Essence. (GOD)

Fear can cause your life to be in endless wonderment about that which you can not see and even can't be looked at, because of the presence of fear in your body eyes, which cause you to be always looking to believe about that which you do not know and is preventing you from seeing that which you need to know, concerning your Life meaning and purpose for being a part of the physical Universe.

It is a fearful life that keep you attached to the Physical, causing you not to be able to ever enter the Metaphysical of Divine Existence, the Dimension where fear does not roam and the Divine Truth and Reality become your Existing companion.

Fear is a mental disease that is equal to the effect of cancer to life, it is out to disqualify the mind from knowing the Divine Truth about life and the way it is meant to be lived.

Fear is always out to keep your life away from the path of harmony, fear being a companion to confusion, the state of mind that prevent you from being able to experience your Divine spirituality, an experience that require Mind (Thought) self control.

Fear is the companion to evil, it is out to prevent your life from being peaceful and joyful with your self, it prevent you from knowing what you need to know and it is knowing with understanding that is capable of conquering fear, it being an ally to lies and cause you to be deceitful in life.

Fear is that duo consisting of lies and deception, that which prevent you from entering the space of Mind that introduce you to the pleasure of Life Divine Spirituality, which is a matter of discipline thought, an order where fear can not reside.

The only Beings amongst us that are justified in expressing the emotion of fear are our children and it is the child that is yet capable of profoundly reasoning the way through life.

Death

Chapter 5

Well, you could be asking, what does death has to do with our Divine Spirituality, well, the same as Life has to do with your Divine Spirituality, because you can't have the experience of one without experiencing the action that cause other, one is physical and the other is not physical and in the not physical, which is the inert ethereal state of existence, there to is where Divine actuality reside.

Existence is a realm that death take you into such a infinite realm and it is where there is no need to remember or forget, on the realm of the body life, divine spirituality is when expressed in the body life, it is an expression of attitude and behavior on the physical level.

The Divine intelligent energy is a Divine action that is not of physical life, it is what causes you to have life, but in death the physical life is not but it is present as well in the eternal state of existence.

The Divine energy is in a constant state of actual existence, it is in life as well as in death, it is to be in the physical and it is in the not to be physical, death is divinely spiritual, without the body physical.

Yet it is each level of expression of your Energy reality, which reveal life and eternal existence, which is in fact complimenting each other, one in the action of being physical and the other being not physical when in the elevation into the realm of the nonphysical.

Divine Reality, which is what death is all death does is to elevate you from the physical to the nonphysical state of eternal infinite existence as it plays out its action in the body life, eliminating the physical and verify the inert ethereal nonphysical eternal state of existence beyond life .

No one know what happen after life, death cause existence to have its own private story and story is not what it is known to be on the physical level of life, it is everything that you do not know about after life.

Death is the elevator that take you to the Soul eternal place of existence, it transform life and Mind back into becoming as it actually is, which is the Soul in its actual unchanging state of eternal infinite existence, being always in and of the bosom of the Divine Essence.

Divine existence resides in the bosom of the Divine Essence, the Divine Essence being the cause for the Eternal Infinite Darkness, To Be.

It is death that introduce you to the Divine existence of the perfect night, It being the Infinite Universe where all things reside in an elemental state of action, which come forth into becoming physically apparent and not being physically apparent, as the Infinite Universe turn.

all action being of the Divine Spiritual Truth and Reality, which is the Perfect Night, the garment of the Divine Essence, the Divine Reality of Death to the illusion of Life, and Life and Death signify, Not To Be, And To Be, one experience is of the spiritual illusionary world and the other is an existence of the ethereal eternal Energy reality, which is Divine infinity.

What is death to life but to bring the energy self of you back into the ethereal energy spiritual realm of eternal infinity, yet we are taught to fear such a deathly phenomena to life, when all death does is allow you to experience the Spirituality of life.

Death allow your body life a Divine experience or a profane experience, you determine which you will experience in life, one is of a physical illusion about reality while the other is the ethereal Divine reality, death being separate and apart from your life physical experience.

so what goes on in the ethereal realm, effectively affect what goes on in the physical realm of Physical Illusion, which cause such a happening to appear to be an actuality occurring only in the physical dimension of your body self, which is not the actual ethereal state of divine nonphysical existence.

In our effort to attain our Divine Spirituality in the physical world, we must master the knowledge of fear and death, they being an actuality to life, allowing life to appear in the physical mental world, which develop and express a spirituality that is unique to life experience.

Because without death, life is not to be, but with death inactive presence, life is as it appear to be, which is a physical material body in a Mental state of Mental motion.

So death to the body is what allows the life of and within the body to be, but death taken away from the body, is what cause life not to be, death being a Divine spiritual experienced happening that can only effect life if Death is presently inactive in life.

Death is a phenomena to life, when inactive it allow life to experience its mental thoughts, but without death inactivity, it will cause life experiences to cease to be and without such life experiences, there will be no need to desire to experience the awareness of the ethereal Dimension.

So while life is present in the Body Mind activity then death become inactive in your life and where there is death active, the body cease to be alive, because in order for life to be, death must remain inactive in and to that body life.

We wonder more so about death than we do about life and such wonderment is what cause us to not know the meaning and purpose of life, preventing us from enjoying the Divinity of life Spirituality.

While you are not realizing that death serve only a meaning and purpose to life that is not present after life is no more, because life is only present on the physical level of your Body-Mind activity.

Life is for the body, death is what cause the soul to remain in the realm of Eternal Infinite existence, the difference being that life is with death and the soul existence is beyond the effect of death happening.

So death is a part of the package of life, you can not have one without the other and it is your life that you have been given charge of and not death, it act in relationship to life, as life has a relationship to death, which it can only manage but not control, because one is in need of the other in order to be efficient in their relationship to each other.

So we must accept death not as a threat to life, but as a certainty to life and when we reach such a Divine Mind maturity, only then will we develop the Divine Spirituality that will allow us to Mentally Ethereal Travel into the various Dimensions of our Life Mind action and See the Divine Truth and Reality about the Divine Essence, about both Universe, and our Life self.

Death is just as a Divine experience than Life is, because Death never lose its Divinity, only in Life do we experience a Life living experience that is different from the Life we were given to experience.

You see, you must come to understand that life as a procedure for living is as Death is, as a procedure for not living, the two expression of action is Divine, in and of the action taking place, it is just that, in Life, there are other components to that action that have to do with the Body-Mind-Spirit.

So those principles of life can and does change, they can represent an expression that is Divine to Life Living or they can represent an expression that is full of what we describe as Evil, an expression of Life that is entirely out of Harmony, Order, and Balance with the Spirit of the Universe.

So you must have an expressed Dynamic relationship with each universal body, which is in Divine relationship with each other, never to interfere with the other in a destructing way, such a discipline is referred to as a Divine Spirituality, an expression that is of and within the Universe action.

Death is the most dependable action to life and yet it is the most feared and unpopular action in life, the least talked about concerning life, when in fact we will never get to know and appreciate Life until we get to know and accept Death as being an intricate part of our lives, we can ignore many things about our lives but death can not be ignored, no matter how intense we attempt to be in doing so.

As I have shared, Death to Life and Life to Death is as Siamese twin, one connected to the other, and as long as the two stay joined together, your life is secure.

So Death is not as mean as we claim it to be, and as long as Life and Death stay joined together in harmony then life has its experiences and advantages and can, if respected and protected by you, be as joyful and peaceful as you protect it to be.

Life come with life responsibilities, which is to keep life connected to Death, because only then are you capable of pursuing Life ambitions and desires, which can take you beyond the perceived notion of life into the conceived awareness of your Ethereal existence.

Such an undertaking, happening within the action of your Divine Spirituality, with Death remaining in its innate ethereal state attached to your Life, is what give life the opportunity to be lived, how you live it, become your responsibility.

I intend for this book to be a book that deal with very interesting subjects in a very nonconforming way, not conforming to the well accepted belief about the popular topics that is a part of our life discussed belief.

so you, the readers of this book can rest assure to know that even you have the freedom to disagree, but if you do, don't let it be for the conventional reason you have been conditioned to believe about life, let it be for profound Divine reason, if so, then you will have no reason to disagree with what is being shared with you in this book..

You are getting information about familiar subjects that is a part of your life discussion, but it is different from what we have been taught to believe, so I do not see the need to be writing about something and not using information that is revealed to me, simply because it does not conform to the norm concerning what you have been told to believe about topics that are of interest to your lives experiences and inexperience.

So, as for as I am concerned, Death is an inexperienced topic that does affect our lives in a way that many of us are afraid to acknowledge today and the reason is the way we have been conditioned to not know, but to believe about Death.

There is to me, nothing more interesting than the subject of death, because it require a very self examination in being truthful with your self, that is if you are to ever come to respect that one familiar phenomena that is a very connective part of life, whether we like it or not, or attempt to fake its Divine Meaning or not.

Because to death, it really does not matter, it is going to play out its role to life regardless of what we have been told to believe about it, and death does require that we take a Divine Spiritual approach about it, that is if we are serious about understanding it, and that is what I am doing to every topic I will address in this book, taking a Divine Spiritual approach to share with you information that can change the way that you view your life spirituality.

So yes, death is a very intricate part of life, even though many untruths have been told and still is being told about death and as I have said, you will not be able to express your Divine Spirituality divinely, not until you learn to deal honestly with death.

Yes, death can be a very complicated topic to deal with if you make it to be, and many things are complicated to us because we will have them to be, by the way we believe about them and not attempt to get to know about them, which require that you use your Mind and not somebody else mind to reason about those made to be complicated things in your life and beyond your life, which you imagine about.

Death should never be imagined about, because when you do, you do to yourself and death a disservice, because most if not all that you are imagining about death, is based upon what you have been taught to believe about death and you can not have a Divine spiritual acquaintance with Death, using your mind to believe about death, you must come to know about death.

We have been conditioned to believe that through death we carry life into another dimension and will have the same sensations we had with life on the physical level of our body dimension, as I have shared with you, Life is only for the body and the moment death dissolve life, then life cease to be and is not transferable, regardless of what you have been conditioned to believe about death and life having a relationship to each other, when in fact life and death has no relationship with each other, only a connection to each other.

Because life and death have two entirely different functions, which is in death there is not life and in life there is not death, because the two can not function in a relationship with each other, their objective is entirely different to life.

You see, life is to be lived and death is to bring an ending to the life-living process and that process is not transferable.

So life is meant to be enjoyed on the physical body level of your life action, because with death performance, it cause life to cease to be and the body it once gave motion to, it fades away to be no more.

So yes, life is a spiritual experience and the quality of such an experience is depended entirely upon death not interfering with the nature and quality of your Spirituality.

Death must remain silent in your life, then it all become depended on how much control you have of your Mind, because by you not having control over your Mind, your spirituality become of the Mind action of those that have control of your Mind.

In life it is your Mind that determine the quality of your Life Spirituality and all such life action will be as long as death stay connected to your life, because the moment death disconnect away from your life, your life cease to be a body living phenomena.

So, why is it do we attempt to take life beyond the threshold of death, because beyond death, life is not to be, only ethereal existence occupy such space of infinity, representing to be the attribute of the Divine Essence, whose existence is Eternity and whose Time is infinity.

The Divine Essence dress wear is the Perfect Night, the Darkness which you have been taught to despise as you claim to desire the comfort of your Divine Spirituality, which can not be, without the knowledge of and the embrace of the Perfect Night, because such an accomplishment will cause you to become knowledgeable of Thyself.

So in life, death is not life enemy, just life companion and by the two connected, life can be as exciting and rewarding as you will have it to be, because only in the body can you enjoy such a life or have such a life to become a menace to the body.

The will of the mind is yours to decide, and choice, well it can be made to be influenced, so choice without will does not make for wise decision for your life.

So here is a question to be asked, is death an experience or is it a finality, because that which is final is no more and take my word, death is not an experience, it is a finality, and to make claim that you have experienced death is only a statement that reveal your confusion concerning death, and no, you can not escape death.

You might be able to escape that which could have caused your death to become a reality to your life, but never do you escape death, because death represent the close down of life experience in the physical body, the transforming of life to not life, no one has entered the domain of death and reappeared back in the same life body that death extracted your life from, white light or not.

Death is the finality of life, meaning that the soul is at a complete shut down in the body and no longer active in the body of life, all organic activity in the body is no longer functioning and as long as the soul sense of mind is active, even when can not be detected, death is still connected to life and the soul has not yet exit the body life, because when it does, there is no coming back to life.

The near end of life experience is not a near death experience and all of that take place in a traumatic life experience to have you to experience a mind end life euphoria experience.

Such an experience is not to be compared to be a death experience, because such is not to be experienced and still is connected to life experience, you can not have life and death happening at the same Time, sorry, that is not the discipline of life and death in connection to each action.

Yes, the so call life near death experience can be referred to as being a spiritual experience because such an experience has to do with the life mind attitude and behavioral expression.

You see, spirituality is a Mind act expression that is not a death behavior, but of life mind behavior, and in death, such a life mind activity does not occur beyond life.

You see, because of our love-hate fascination with death, we end up ascribing much to death that is not within the bound of sound rational reasoning, we have been trained to believe that death is an experience and that life has a place after death disconnect from life, causing life to be no more in the physical body, it is such a belief about life and death that prevent you from being able to experience your Divine Spirituality.

We are led to believe about death as if it is some kind of skeletal grim looking creature that come knocking on your life door, with the intent of reaping your life from your body, when in fact death is already in your life house and it is only life circumstance that cause death to exit the house of your life, causing your body to become without its life motion.

In Divine Spirituality, death is a compliment to life, as life is an acknowledgement to death, the body not being able to acknowledge death without experiencing life.

Soul

Chapter 6

The soul is a term we use without thinking about it, because of the fact what we have been told about it in a doctrinal institution we call religion which teaches us to believe that the primary purpose of life is for us to save our soul.

So right off the bat it is implied that the soul is a part of our life activity and that because we are Human Beings in our body life living you are born to sin and is shaped in iniquity, a teaching of religion.

So we immediately believe that there is nothing about life that come here in a good and Divine fashion and that we are born to lie and deceive each other and to persuade each other that there amongst the anthropomorphous

Beings are certain groups of people that are born to be superior over others, based solely on the pigment of your skin and mannerism.

Those people are identified and classified to be lesser people and they are taught to accept those people who have declared themselves superior over Human Beings with a Corporeal nature and have been placed in a lower class of society.

Those Human Beings who have come to be in charge of society, they have caused there to be a social class system and within that system is born a lower class standard within that society.

The lower class of society are force to have a lower living standard in life and to be the declared inferior people by the master teacher of religion, teaching the doctrine of religion concerning God, Universe, self, and in the civil and religious society is taught the way people of those societies must behave in life.

So it is as if our life is preordained and predestined, not by God, but by people who have readily confessed to be born Human Beings who are born in Sin and is shaped in iniquity.

In other word, to be superior over certain ethnic groups of people with one group in their Mind in particular being to those certain people of a society that is divided into social class, the superior class in the civil as well as the religious society are confessed liars and deceivers.

Those people that has a shade of pigment that is as Black as Night, they are also with a soul, but is treated as if to be without a soul and Black as they are, society is taught to believe that they are evil and is not to be respected.

All because they are people who you have been taught to believe is inferior to people with a soul that has a fair (light) pigment.

We are also told by the teaching of a religious doctrine that the Soul is in need of being saved and that some souls more so than others of the Human Being lighter (White) Race is more important than others who are not white.

Society is taught to believe that those people who are with a darker pigment, they come with a condemned soul, and they are not fully Human Beings, all because of the shade of their pigment.

Those who made such a claim about Black people not being Human Beings and those making such a claim did so without realizing, by them making such an assertion about Black people, they were in fact telling the Truth about Black people not being Human Beings, because they came to this planet being Divine Beings with a Divine Soul, without the student of such a doctrine knowing it.

Because the Dark as night people was in fact produced as Divine Beings and were produced in equal fashion to all other Beings, there came a time when those Beings were taken advantage of and they lost their Divinity and were mentally conditioned to become Human Beings, they with a mind that lie and deceive, claiming to have a superior soul.

So, let us see what the soul really is and whether or not it is in need of religious saving.

The Soul of all Beings, regardless of their phenotype, form, and shape, they are all with a soul and it most certainly is not in need of being saved.

It is the Soul of the Being that cause the Being to have a body life, because it is the soul that is the Core energy of the body life and it is what provide the Divine Energy for your body life to be in motion.

The soul is the energy center that provide energy throughout the body life, it is to the body that which cause the body to be the life Being that you are, a Being with a life that is in motion only because of your soul, a soul that is not in need of being saved not by anybody of this planet earth.

The soul is what makes you to be what your life is, which is a body with a mind that is in motion and how you live your life is entirely up to you, without a threat coming from God dictating how you are to live your life.

The soul is liken to the Core of the earth, it is the energy organ of the earth, which generate a gravitational magnetic field for the earth from within, which is why the Core of the earth is the Soul of the earth and so it is within your Body.

So, to you the anthropomorphous Being that is calling yourselves Human Beings, it is your Soul that is your energy source for your body life.

The soul is what preserve and inform your life and not your life having authority over the Soul, the soul being that which cause your body to be in motion, it being the divine energy used to provide to you life, as has been stated to you early on in this chapter.

The divine soul is the source that provide the Metaphysical information about the inner self existence and is what give cause for the outer body self appearing intelligent.

The soul is based upon the soul sense to mind developed interaction, with the Mind being no more than an extension of the Soul action providing to the body life the ability to thoughtful reason and I will go more into the Mind relationship to the Soul in the chapter that will be about the Mind, but right now let me share with you more about the Soul.

It is the Energy of the Soul over which and through which all information flow to the body life mind and it is that energy source, the soul, that can not be persuaded nor can it be influenced by your body life action.

The soul is what cause your body to have life and life is motion, but how you choose to live your life, it is not the responsibility of the soul, nor is it the persuasion of the soul, the divine energy that persuade not.

It is the soul that is in a preserved place in the body, the center of your body, which is the organ we call the Brain, therein rest the pineal gland, the energy source to the body life, yet the soul is not a part of the brain organ, it is the generator of energy to that organ the brain.

There is what is referred to as a pineal Gland in the body brain, yet it can not be easily gotten to nor can it be extracted with surgical instruments, because the pineal Gland is the provider and generator of electrical impulse that is flowing throughout the brain and to its body nerve cord giving the body the ability to be in motion, the Pineal Gland being the energy provider to the body life.

There is not much to be explained about the soul, yet it is the central source, the core, the essence of your body life, just as the Divine Essence is to the Soul of all things that move and move not, and things that can be looked at and things that can not be looked at, the soul is the central action of life and most certainly is not in need of being saved.

So, it is the soul of your body Being, that provide your life with the ability to have Will and to make Choices for your Life way to live, it is the soul that maintain the body equilibrium , it is what cause the body rotation on its axis , and the Mind, it is what keeps your body life revolving in the space where your life live.

Remember, without the Soul, your Life cease to be and the body dissolve away, not to be alive any more within the body, the soul is the me that cause the self to be the I, revealing the trinity of the body you, in action, that trinity being the soul sense, mind, and spirit of your body action.

I know, yes so much have been told to you about the soul and having you to believe that what is told to you about the soul is true and you are to believe with faith and hope and not to use thought to reason about what is told to you about the soul.

You see, it is the soul that is as God is to the body and you being in motion become the evidence that the soul is there in the body, but it not being able to be seen or touched, it only give cause for the body to be a potential intelligent life Being, with the ability to reason and make decision for your life.

SHOW ME A MIND THAT DOES NOT MAKE DECISIONS FOR THE LIFE IT GUIDE AND I WILL SHOW YOU A BEING THAT IS NOT IN CONTROL OF ITS LIFE AND WHEN THE BODY, MIND, AND SPIRIT, IS NOT IN HARMONY WITH THE INFORMATION FLOWING FROM THE SOUL, THEN IT WILL NOT BE ABLE TO EXPERIENCE DIVINE SPIRITUALITY.

IT IS THE SOUL THAT PROVIDE INFORMATION ABOUT THE INNER SELF AS WELL AS ABOUT THE OUTER BODY SELF, CONCERNING LIFE HAPPENINGS, THAT WHICH IS OCCURRING NOW, AND ABOUT THAT WHICH HAVE HAPPEN BEFORE, AND ABOUT THINGS THAT

ARE HAPPENING THAT IS BEYOND THE BODY
LIFE PRESENT EXPERIENCE.

IT IS THE SOUL ACTION WHICH IS TAKING
PLACE WITHIN THE SPACE OF YOUR ETHEREAL
INNER SELF EXISTENCE, WITH ITS ETERNAL
CLOAK BEING THE INFINITE DARKNESS, THE
ETERNAL DIVINE ESSENCE DOMAIN AND IS
THE DOMINION OVER ALL THINGS THAT ARE
AND ARE NOT, SUCH IS THE ACTION THE SOUL
IS PROVIDING TO THE BODY LIFE AND THE
SOUL IS LIKEN TO THE DIVINE ESSENCE TO
ALL THINGS PHYSICAL AND IS NOT PHYSICAL.

It is the duty of the mind to listen to the soul and not
to save the soul, because it is the soul that is capable
of giving your mind the ability to save your life and I
have shared with you in this book, that life is for the
body and it is because of the soul being your body life
essence and it being that which need not to be saved by
the action of your body life, is what make the soul to be
the center of your body life action.

It is the soul that reside in a state of eternal infinite
existence, it is the entity of the Divine Essence, WHICH
IS THE CAUSE FOR THE SOUL TO BE, WHETHER
ITS ACTION IS TAKING PLACE IN YOUR LIFE
OR OUT BEYOND YOUR LIFE ACTIVITIES, THE
SOUL REMAIN TO BE THE DIVINE ENERGY
THAT PROVIDE LIFE TO YOUR BODY AND
THROUGHOUT BOTH UNIVERSE.

Mind – Heart

Chapter 7

First allow me to share with you information been told about the heart, information most of us use and accept as fact without thinking, because it is an approved religious assertion that there is such a member of the body referred to as the heart other than the organ heart member of the body.

We go about our daily lives using such a term as heart, indicating that it can be used to amplify and magnify our sense life activities, by expressing the highest quality of our life emotion.

We have been led to believe when it is not, that emotion is an entity of life expression by a heart that is different from the heart that pump the fluid throughout our body, used to help sustain our body life, well I am here to share with you that the body life carry only one heart, the organ pump that is of and in the body, pumping the fluid of life therein.

There is now the claim that it has been scientifically discovered that there are three entities of brain heart like activity in our body, they each having a magnetic field of its own, that cause you to generate an electrical impulse to give to you the ability to do such things as love, to be sentimental, to have compassion, and all of those body sensations that give you the ability to care with passion emotion.

There is also the saying that there is a magnetic field that reside in the brain like solar plexus (gut) of your body and it to, give off the ability for you to have the urges you have for each other, in a very special and intimate way, thus giving us the pyramid effect of a body life of passionate emotion that is different from our sense emotion and feeling, giving off a three brain like effect to your body life.

Well again I share with you that in the body anatomy there is only one brain, one heart, and one soul, and it is the organ heart that pump with harmonic vibration the fluid of life through out our body.

All of the passion and urges of desire and our ability to reason, all such action is taking place in the energy that flow from the central location of our body life, which we refer to as being the brain, and that energy is compartmentalized by the way the mind function.

Not until there become the ability to actuate that energy mind in such a way until it develop what we consider to be the thoughts of our body life revealing the kind of emotion that is contributed to the heart, when in fact those emotions are generated by the mind, so you love with your mind and not the heart.

The mind is the energy field that incorporates, integrate, separate and formulate that energy that is flowing in and from the brain to form the ethereal entity we refer to as being the mind.

It is the mind, which is no more than thought, that receive and interpret the energy that flow from the soul to the brain that give the body life the ability to reason, rationalize, and to be logical in our action of expression, which is displayed by our body life action, the spirit of the body life.

The mind is what is call expressive thought, so as I share with you here, it is the mind that is your every thought and reveal your every emotion, no matter how you choose to express it in your body life activity.

The energy that is flowing to and through your body life hard drive, the brain, the central headquarter of your body life, it is there from, where the spirit of your life emanate at will, from a developed mind which you refer to as being the hear from which is expressed your emotions.

There may be some things revealed in this book that may be repeated and if so, just know it is done to make sure it is in this book for you to receive as you so desire to study carefully and come to understand clearly.

Below is a quote which I am sharing with you, it is in an effort to prove to you that the body has two Hearts, one for the body and the other for our own created use, which I disagree with, and no doubt as you continue to read, you will see why I do.

Here are the quotes below, a claim about the heart coming from somebody other than myself, to you the reader:

"MYTH: The brain is the source of all human Intelligence".

"FACT: Your highest intelligence comes from at

"Least three different brains and you need them

 Working together. "

"Neuroscientists have

Found a second true brain in the gut (the

"Enteric nervous system," with more than 100

Million neurons) and another one inside the

Heart, which radiates feelings up to 10 feet

Away and is the primary source of motivation

Trust, and loyalty."

"By the way, 40 to 50 percent

of the fluctuations in an organization's profit

Margin is predictable based on people

Feelings and opinions — so these other brains

Also have huge financial implications" end of quote.

Now, the primary source that cause the body to have life is the soul of the body and the soul really indicate the central theme of life being Energy that flow throughout the body and it is the Mind that is established by the Soul which give the body its sense of purpose.

The brain is just an organ of the body life, it is the distribution center for the soul, it send out energy waves throughout the body brain, activating the various organ centers in the body and it is the Soul energy that is capable of revealing information to give the body life.

All of the body life information is coming from the soul of the body, revealed by the Soul Mind, nothing in the field of consciousness happens, that is expressed by the body, without it first been revealed by the soul to the body mind, nothing.

The body Soul energy is the source of the body intelligence, the mind reveal that intelligence, regardless of its quality of expression by the sense –mind interaction that is revealed by the body indicated action.

Feeling is of the sense- mind interaction, it being an energy impulse expression, revealed by the spirit expressed by the body life, the spirit being the expressed attitudinal behavior of the body life which is conducted by the sense-mind action.

The sense mind action is what come from the cause of the action of the body life soul, which is the energy source of the body, the intelligence expressed by the mind by the body life action, all of which is caused by the body soul and it being compartmentalized and distributed throughout the body, causing the body to come alive and all such soul information being received and interpreted by the mind.

Even with our well renowned spiritualist and religious theologians, the use of the term heart by them is told to you to be the way to verify the depth of your emotional feeling about somebody or something.

It is commonly suggested to you by your leaders whom you hold to high respect, they claiming that when ever you do something from the use of the heart, then you are being sincere, you are being godly, and is showing a religious spirit.

What ever you do they tell you, do it from the heart, which heart, certainly not the heart our organ, if not, then which, and what is the procedure for which it is to become a part of your body life economy ?

The Heart, second to God, is the most lied about created entity by the Human Beings that has ever been expressed to be the instrument to use to express sincerity, meekness and repentance to each other.

The Human Beings, they who have religiously claimed to have been born in sin and is shaped iniquity, being an imperfect Being which they claim to be, they are those who have gotten you to use a term of expression that is not a part of your body economy.

So any process of the body life that is not an affixed organ or limb that is of the body life, is a fake when a claim of something being associated to the body, using the term of a body organ but is not, then know that is not true.

All of that is a fake, being used to determine the quality of your life emotional expressed action and is not capable of assisting you in reaching your Divine Spiritual potential in life.

In life it is your Divine Spirituality (attitudinal behavior) and not your religious spirituality (believing Heart) that is capable of elevating your life living to that which is of a Divine quality, revealing a Divine Spiritual life expression.

It is such a quality of Divine Spiritual life expression where evil is not present and is not allowed in your life Divine expressed activities, that is what gives to your life a Divine meaning.

The Human Being has created the term heart and all of those other terms of words and gave to them their meaning and that is why I am not bounded to honor them and I can assign my own meaning to the various aspect of the expression of the body life and include it to be natural as well.

It is Divine to be able to express emotions that come from the process of Divine thought to put on display your Divine Spirituality, knowing the reward benefit, that come from being in such an expressed Divine spirit.

Many use their religious belief to serve as a sign of their spirituality and to do it, then the use of belief become such an expression in life that is not a natural label for your life emotional expression, making religious belief to be more of the heart than of the Divine Mind.

The heart of passion is no more than a misrepresentation of the body life expression, claiming that such is the cause for its emotional function, and it is the heart that is given credit for a body life expressed emotion.

The heart as we know it to be, it can not produce, it is the spirit expressed emotion being revealed by the mind action that reveal your spirituality, which the heart can not do in the body life, only through the soul sense-mind action, it can be done.

In religious spirituality, it is taught that such a life elevated spiritual experience, must come from the heart, not distinguishing which heart, as if it is more than one, and if so, it is a made up entity that has a classification and an identity described as a life expressed religious behavioral spirit of emotion and not a Divine mind spiritual emotion.

It is the religious heart that is based upon expressed belief in life and it is the Divine mind that reveals an expressed knowledge about life.

It is a common accepted notion that we must do everything in life while claiming the heart is the main source you should use to express your seriousness and devotion about your loving and caring of others in life.

What you are doing and how you are doing it is determined by the quality of not the heart but the mind, because the heart is what maintains life while the mind determines the quality of your life.

Our Divine highest expression of our feeling must be made known and is done so by the mind and not the heart, so in order for our feeling to be of the sincere quality that we claiming it must be, then it is the mind and not the heart that make it to be so.

It is the heart that we describe our feeling from, but it is the mind that verifies our thoughts in expressing emotions we have for some one or something done by expressing a Divine spirit.

The heart is a claimed described expression given to be uncontrollable and irrational, while the Divine mind is controllable and rational, in its emotional expression.

To make a Claim that the heart is a representation of deep sincere emotion capable of causing you to express yourself in a truthful emotional way is done by habit and it show that the statement is more based upon emotion than the fact of the matter concerning the purpose of the "Heart" is to the Body life..

While you claiming the heart to be your center of verified quality of emotional expression, again, where and what dynamic relationship does the heart hold, in and to the body life other than to be the body organ that pump the blood of life throughout the body.

There is nothing that is done to express emotion demonstrated by the body action without the action of your mind and it is your mind that is, because of your brain action that serve to be the true expression of your spirit.

Your mind being an ethereal associated attribute to the soul of your body life, the energy that send information throughout the body life, with the mind formed to receive and to reveal all information that is pertained to the body life emotional state.

So there is not one thing that happen in an expressed way, coming from the body life, without the functional action of those brain waves we call the mind, as we substitute it to be what we claim to be the heart, not realizing, that emotion it is not to have relevant meaning without the Mind.

It is with the mind that we give the body life sense its effective meaning to the body life and only through the sense-mind coordination you are able to experience the effect the senses have to the body.

It is in actuality the senses through which the mind is capable of demonstrating the expression of the body spirit which reveal the emotional effect coming from the body action.

Without the mind and not the heart, there would not be an effective way to express the spirit of our thoughts because only with our sense to mind action we are able to think, see, smell, hear, taste, and feel.

So it is the mind that is the revealing action of the body life emotions, which make it to be six senses of the mind that reveal the emotional state of body life action.

It is the brain that serves as the soul energy distributor throughout the body life, meaning in actuality the body life is all energy and without the soul the body life become acquainted with death.

Death to the body life does cause the absent of life in the body, which cause the elements, water, air, heat and earth particle, which cause the body to have form and life, to dissolve back into its ethereal elemental state of existence, back into the perfect eternal infinite night, it being the Divine Essence to all things that are not and is to be.

We to much, take our mind for granted, assigning its performance to something we have created for ourselves, calling it the heart, not realizing that there is not one thing associated to the body life expression that the mind is not in charge of to give it meaning, revealing by your body action your life spirit.

It is the mind that is a member of the body life trinity which cause the body to be able to be alive, that trinity being the soul, brain, and mind, the three being in all actuality, ONE, and not until you are qualified to see that truth, you will not be qualified to experience the Divine quality of the Mind, which is what cause you to be able to experience your Divine Spirituality.

The Kundalini:

"Kundalini is the Hindu word for the "sacred transformative energy that awakens consciousness", "the coiled," or the "Serpent power".

I will throughout this book use very simple recognized terms to reveal the meaning and inner most action that take place outside as well as inside of the body life.

Take for instance the word kundalini, which is just another word in another language for energy, the sacred inheritance of the body life, without it, life in the body will cease to be, with it, the body life has the potential of becoming an intelligent Being.

The all important thing to the body life and to have an understanding of that life, is for us to first know and understand the energy that flow throughout the body life, and the many roles the energy cause the body life to be able to perform, be it outside and inside the body life, it is the energy of the body that cause the body to be alive.

Within the body life, it is the energy that provide the body life the ability to perform, such a performance is taking place through what is referred to as the Mind, which is not a material object of the body but it is an ethereal immaterial action of the body, which give meaning to the body life.

It is the mind that cause all action of the body, which is generated by the soul energy, which give the body life the ability to do what we call to think, reason, analyze, know, understand, dream and have visions, to name just a few acts of the mind.

It is the mind that is able to reach conclusions about information received from the Soul which has a sense to mind relationship, information that is absorbed to be the assimilated truth and reality we expressively identify what we deem truth and reality to be, which is a part of our body life recognized action.

So in all actuality information is happening and coming within the energy flow to our established mind and it is the mind that is the immaterial matter entity of the body life and it is the mind that reveal compartmental dimensions from which life expressions are experienced.

All of our expression is an act of the mind and not the heart which is revealed in the action of our spirit and is acted out by the body life, that is how we get to express our spirituality that is coming from our mind action, as all things that effect us is revealed and expressed by our mind through our body life action.

Within the corridors of the Mind there are many compartments in where things of different function is going on, it is as if the mind act as a sifter to the kundalini. (energy)

Information come to us by way of energy waves, which flow to establish a mind like sensation and it give a mental confirmation in order to be able to formulate a conscious awareness for the outer body life to act upon.

Energy information is as well for the inside body organs and the combination of the two action is what give the body life, and its life meaning and purpose for being.

All for you to know and understand the interaction between the outer and inner action of the body life, using all of the body attributes, which is the soul, body, mind, sense, spirit, with the body organs representing the action of the body life inner action.

That is what gives purpose to the body life, with the soul-mind being the guiding and revealing source of and to the body life.

DIMENSIONS OF THE MIND:

The mind is the extension of the soul, it is a function that interact with the physical and the metaphysical, with the mind having the ability to reveal to you the going on that is happening outside of you as well as inside of your self.

It is the mind that is being able to render dreams and visions about things that have happened on the outside of you, as well as what have happened to you, and is happening beyond you on the inside of you.

The mind reveal to you things about you that has happened and is happening to you on the physical level, as those things are revealed by the sense mind interaction and what is revealed by the mind, is that which is happening on the physical as well as the ethereal level of your self physical dimension.

It is the Mind that is able to have you see what is happening in the metaphysical dimension, that dimension which is revealed by the mind on the conscious and subconscious level of the body life action, as things are revealed to you causing you to know about present and past life happenings.

The ethereal Truth and Reality is an action that take place beyond life experiences, past and present, and it is that action that is happening beyond the conscious levels of the mind action, and therefore on such a level, there is the happening revealed by the intuitive action of your ethereal self, some people refer to it as the spirit self.

The mind is so intimately related to the soul until it equally is the esoteric aspect of the body life, but it is not a material organ attachment to your life.

The Mind is the ethereal instrument of the body that reveal the quality of intelligence of the type of Being that you are, it is the mind that reveal your life experiences in a way you can appreciate and enjoy or it can deflate your life in a way you will despise. Yet it is your mind that has the power to cause your life to be as you so will it to be.

The mind is what produce and reveal the spirit of your life, the mind can be liken to being the god of your life, while the soul being the goddess of your mind, one feed while the other one partake in the receiving of that which is in constant feed, coming from the soul to the mind.

The mind is what cause the body life to have meaning and purpose, giving the body life the spiritual (attitudinal behavior) power of having Will and Choice, Will being the power capable of having the body life to be able to experience the Greater Good that it is capable of causing your life to enjoy.

Such a quality of life experience can only be caused by your mind and not by the action of an illusionary life in the sky.

So, within the frame work of your mind and if it is functioning Divinely, it is qualified to reveal to you dimensions of activity that is beyond your life pay grade to experience, those are dimensions that dwell beyond the mind life ability to travel and see.

so that is why the body life is equipped with a three dimensional self, one sensual physical, one mental spiritual, and one soulful intuitively, which is an action that take place in the body that is not sensual nor mental, it is the Dimension where your Divine essence, the soul reside.

The Divine intuitive self is in the eternal infinite space of the dark core of your soul body life, the soul being the goddess of the nonphysical and is beyond your body life experience

Your intuitive self inform you of the physical exoteric happening and the metaphysical esoteric happening of your physical and non physical self, absent of mind conscious involvement.

Not until we are qualified to master the knowledge of our Soul-mind interactive relationship, we will not be qualified to be able to experience the Greater Good of what our body life is in possession of that can be revealed to us, it being a life mind quality that is capable of producing the Divine spirituality that your life is entitle to enjoy.

There is a movie that was produced by the title, the Matrix, a movie if you are intelligently spiritual enough, will have your mind in attention to what it was conveying about society and its influence upon your mind, leading you to know that if you do not control your mind, anybody can control your life.

So here is a short piece of the quotes from some one other than myself, coming from the movie, the matrix.

So my comments will be intertwined below the quotes and is without the quote symbol.

"Matrix Quotes Unearth Facts About Reality and Illusion,

For some, The Matrix is just another sci-fi movie, a slick production from Hollywood's dream factory. But for those who appreciate the philosophy of The Matrix, it is a wake-up call. The movie is considered to be far-ahead of its times. It challenges our understanding of perspective, reality and illusion, and many other intriguing concepts.

These Matrix quotes are words of wisdom by Morpheus, Neo's spiritual leader and guide."

Morpheus Quotes

"Fate, it seems, is not without a sense of irony."

So it is.

"What is "real"?

"How do you define real"?

Real is not meant to be defined, it is to be acknowledged and verified by your mind ability to divinely reason concerning life.

"This is your last chance. After this, there is no turning back. You take the blue pill -- the story ends, you wake up in your bed and believe whatever you want to believe. You take the red pill -- you stay in Wonderland and I show you how deep the rabbit-hole goes."

A Divine mind does not participate in belief; a Divine mind is the endlessness of knowing, to believe, it limit the mind, but to know, the mind become the infinite rabbit hole.

"I'm trying to free your mind, Neo. But I can only show you the door. You're the one that has to walk through it."

This book, Divine Spirituality, is written for one specific purpose, which is to free the reader mind, because without such a mental freedom, you prevent your self from experiencing your Divine Spirituality, the choice is the reader to make, concerning what type of condition that you will have your mind to experience, as you continue to read this book.

"Have you ever had a dream, Neo, that you were so sure was real"?

"What if you were unable to wake from that dream, Neo"?

"How would you know the difference between the dream world and the real world"?

Dreams are a reflection of an un-imaginary world, could that be your mind reality, which is without your conscious doing?

The mind is capable of taking you into the dream world, to show you a reality of the mind action, having nothing to do with your life mind experience that you are having in the physical world. So what is it that becomes the illusion of reality or is it by the mind action that such things are happening in life that can be label as being real?

It is the mind that give you the ability to choose between what is real and what is not, your life is now and is not beyond your life, it is the Mind we must learn to respect and master with knowledge and understanding and not belief.

"The Matrix is the world that has been pulled over your eyes to blind you from the truth."

The truth is that which only the mind is capable of seeing, the world blind the mind, while having your life eye to sense and look at what you can not see, because the world has become the matrix shield that has been pulled over your mind eye.

"What you know you can't explain, but you feel it. You've felt it your entire life, that there's something wrong with the world. You don't know what it is, but its there, like a splinter in your mind, driving you mad."

What you know you must be capable of explaining that which you do not know, and yet you claim to believe you know, that is what trouble the mind and it is that something that dwell beyond the mind that cause you to know that something is wrong about the world, and it is that which dwell beyond the mind that come to serve as a splinter to your mind, it driving you mad at what you see to be the world evil doing, while you have the Matrix shield which is the world having your mind fall prey to the looking sense of your mind sense eye, the eye of illusion and not the eye of the mind that see know and understand the concept of reality.

"Unfortunately, no one can be told what the Matrix is. You have to see it for yourself."

Only with the Mind under your life control, you are capable of seeing what the Matrix is, it is the world illusions, its curtain that it keep pulled over your Mind eye, preventing you from seeing the reality of the world ways, you must master control of your mind and you will be able to see your way, the way that lead to your life experiencing the Greater Good that your Divine mind has to offer to your life.

"If real is what you can feel, smell, taste and see, then 'real' is simply electrical signals interpreted by your brain."

Real is not what the sense provide to your life, all that is of the sense is an illusion.

Real is what reside beyond the life experiences of your senses and is concealed within the Mind, which give to you the ability to conceive what is real.

So all that live is with life that is caused by electrical impulse, it is not the sense that determine what is real, it is the Mind, the mind it is that reflect the action of the brain action, making the center of your life action to be the soul of your Being.

It is the soul that is the essence of your Mind reality, there is nothing organic that is real, and it is the mind that serves as the prime attribute of the soul, to your life.

"The Matrix is a system, Neo. That system is our enemy. But when you're inside, you look around, what do you see, Businessmen, teachers, lawyers, carpenters"?

"The very minds of the people we are trying to save".

"But until we do, these people are still a part of that system and that makes them our enemy. You have to understand, most of these people are not ready to be unplugged. And many of them are so inert, so hopelessly dependent on the system that they will fight to protect it."

The World is a system locked in the Matrix of its sensuality, it is an enemy to your mind, it seek to guide and control you by the sense of your physical perception, so what you do, you crave and strive for the material things the world offer.

Conspicuous consumption is your goal in life wants, and the world has succeeded in having a lock down of your mind and the victims of the world, the people that make up the world, they are infested with the system of the world, which is vainly selfish, evil, and you do not desire to become unplugged from the world matrix.

All because it will require you to reclaim your Divine mind and a spirituality that will cause you to be able to see the world as it is.

So the people this book aim to help, is and will become an enemy to what this book is revealing to you, simple because it contain information that does not conform to the teaching of those that control the Matrix, the world that have your Mind to go blind.

Yet you claim to be in search for your Divine Spirituality, when in fact, you are a prisoner to the Matrix World religious spirituality, a world that is mentally blind and can not know and see what is Divinely Real and True, outside of the world matrix.

"There is a difference between knowing the path and walking the path."

There is no difference in knowing the path and understanding the path, the both require the use of your Divine Mind, the act that lead you to be able to experience your Divine Spirituality, that which will allow you to walk the path that lead to Divine Revelation about life.

Study the spirit (attitude and behavior) of the Universe and get to know thyself.

Again, the author comments above concerning the Matrix quotes, are without the quote symbol.

CLAIRVOYANCE:

The intuitive self, it is the inner ethereal self energy that perform and inform beyond the conscious and unconscious mind, it is that intuitiveness within the body that perform, informing you about things of happening that is without the help of the mind state of consciousness.

There are many tasks your mind life perform that is revealed by the two levels of consciousness, using the process of thought, but it is the intuitive self, which is not like it is a material object, or a physical organ of your body life, nor is it like the conscious mind, yet it is the ethereal organ inside of the body that is beyond conscious self, acting out its role in your body life, a life that is no more than electrical currents generating responses that is demonstrated by the body for revealing and expressive action.

In the body, there is the constant action of the soul (energy) and it is the brain organ that is receiving the soul energy and spontaneously there become an ethereal manifestation we call the intuitive self whose presence is not always readily known to be present in your body life, it act freely without the governance of the mind level of consciousness, it is the Divine soul intuitive power of your inner ethereal self, revealing to you happenings that is beyond your conscious awareness.

It is the intuitive self that reveal information to you that is coming from the soul brain interaction, delivering information through the brain electrical impulse that is given to you without the involvement of the conscious mind, information about things that happened or is to happen through a vision that is intuitive and not mental, you call such a presence of an inner action, clairvoyance discernment and not conscious awareness

Clairvoyance is an ability to become aware of something that is not revealed by the conscious mind that perform in an informative thoughtful and un-thoughtful but conscious way, where believing or knowing is commonly demonstrated by the mind state of consciousness, things that are revealed by the senses to the body mind, generating an awareness of information displayed by the body life action, the mind being not the pivotal point in this phenomenal of this action that is revealing what the mind is not conscious of, your intuitive self I am referring to here.

The mind is the ethereal self in your body life and by its action it is capable of performing various feats, such as dreaming and mental vision of things that is a part of your past and present life, an action performed on the conscious and unconscious mental level of the sense to mind action.

But your intuitive self is beyond the mind action, it is that little silent voice that show you things and warn you of things without you ever having to think about the things that your intuitive self reveal to you.

 The reason being the performed informative non-mental act that is made manifest by the body physical outward display, conducted by the soul-brain intuitive internal ethereal self that is informing you about the esoteric metaphysical revelation, it is that none mental action that is revealing to you information, without the conscious mind needing to process that intuitive information that is coming from the ethereal inner self.

You know, that little Divine silent voice we all have developed a habit of ignoring because we had nothing to do with how that information we are receiving that apply to our body life got to us without the action of our mind.

It is such a phenomena display of action by the intuitive self, that which consist of the body economy of life on the physical spiritual level, but reveal its intuitive self only on the ethereal nonphysical and esoteric internal level, of your body life.

Such a level being the body physical level in which is being the performance of the intuitive self, showing you things and telling you things that is beyond the conscious mind to know.

The intuitive self does not need the use of the body sense to mind action in order to do what the mind is incapable of doing, which is to demonstrate non physical qualities within the body life and yet does provide information that do not come from the mind, but from your intuitive self, which is call having the gift of being clairvoyance.

It is the inner ethereal intuitive self that be revealing those happenings that is occurring on the metaphysical ethereal level, an action that is demonstrated to be many time metaphorically and is esoterically revealed while under the gifted use of clairvoyance.

Things that are revealed by the mind is not the same thing that is shown by the intuitive self and one of those life mind phenomena is referred to as being when the mind is capable of mentally seeing things that are ethereally happening and is happening on the mental physical body life level.

It is the mental esoteric revelation that is referred to as the phenomena of clairvoyance, a dimension within the body life that is divinely intuitive and such does not require a mental action to put the physical and the metaphysical in such a divine mental state before the past and the present can be shown to you as if you are watching a movie without the use of the mind.

You call that intuitive revelation using the gift of clairvoyance, qualifying you to be able to see what did happen and what is happening and is about to happen, all taking place in the alternation of PAST AND PRESENT, TIME BEING REVEALED THAT IS NOT A SHOW OF JUST YOUR IMMEDIATE LIFE ACTION BUT OF MANY PAST TIME LIFE ACTION OF WHICH YOU ARE A PART OF THOSE LIVES DNA.

Now, how do we enter such a non-mental corridor extending beyond your mind, where such a revelation is coming from a part of your body life action, that has nothing to do with your mind action, you may be wondering, does it take a special type of a person in order to have clairvoyance experienced revelation ?

Well yes, and such a qualification is that you must be of a Divine spirituality that is functioning with divine quality, which mean that every aspect of your mind action must be functioning in Harmony, Order, Balance, with the triad of your body life, they being the Soul, Brain Mind action, having an organic presence serving as the receptor and distributor in this spiritual trinity of an interaction that take place in the body life.

that trinity of action being the soul energy, the brain and the mind energy, and the spirit become the result of those action, yet there within the depth of the soul, there always be the functioning of the intuitive self, functioning independent to the soul, brain, mind action.

Divine Energy, that which is the source in this transference of action to the brain, making the three, the brain, mind, and spirit performances, to be One source of active energy, with the energy being the one and only central motivator in that triad of those performances, the divine energy remaining to be its singularity causing your intuitive action to make you to be clairvoyance.

Yet to all things with a Divine Quality, there is require an intelligence of comparable quality, meaning that there is a technique and a process required in order to accomplish what you set out to do in life, it being done with the use of the mind and not mind, such presence being the central component of your body life.

Many refer to the use of such a ritual that is referred to as Meditation, (which I will address more in depth later on in this book) in an effort to bring into focus, Spiritual Harmony, which require the triad use of the Divine energy performance, that will put you in the metaphysical esoteric world of many mental dimensions, revealing action of past and present experiences of the lives you consist of today.

You may wonder why I have not used the term and tense of Time we call the Future, well in my mind the past and present is the tense of Time that is verifiable, they consist of the actuality of your body life experiences, but the future is an imaginary tense of Time that has yet to become apart of your Mind reality in the physical, as well as in the metaphysical world, Such is of the illusionary and ethereal anticipated Time, and has not yet become a part of the physical world.

So when dealing with the future, meaning not yet happened, you can only imagine what is to happen as oppose to know what already has happened, through the use of your intuitive self having the gift of clairvoyance ability.

To subscribe to there being a future that can be visit by you, and you being in the present and have been of the past, that is to suggest ignorantly that the present and past is only an illusion, but it is the future that is the imaginary dimension and what is imagined to be our future is to become our physical reality, taking place in the present to move on to become the past.

Clairvoyance claim to be able to see into all three direction of time dimensions, well, that I will leave with you the reader to ponder over, me, I will deal in this book with the two actuality of Time as I see it to be and as it apply to the body life experience, which is of the past and present in that progression of Time, which life is related to.

Life is no more than motion, and it also is referred to being Time, and life in relationship to Time, become the same in each of its action, by indicating it to be a period of life experience of the now and before now, the past and present, which is the reminder of life moving experiences which is no fantasy.

I have told you that I will not subscribe to the status quo way of believing, nor will I conform to the established belief we hold about all things that apply to our lives, I am a Divine Free Thinker, sharing with you what has been revealed to me by the Divine Essence, through, from, and by, my Divine Cosmic First Way Ancient Ancestors, it all is happening in a way that it is coming from the energy of my Mind.

Everything we do, we contribute to our body Life and we give our body life experiences, labels, classifications, and categories of descriptions of all of those actions, and all of such applied action appear to be our body life reality and truth, which is a verification of the powerful phenomena of the Mind energy intelligent ability to create our body life reality, it being only an illusion of what in life density we hold to be the body life truth and reality.

There is on the level of our body life density, privileges attributed to be for our body life and we classify such privileges to be the rights, freedom and independence and such is to be enjoyed by tour body life.

Therefore I take such a claim about our body life to associate that there is to be a body life action when being Divine, to have the ability to be clairvoyance and to see and know things that is not of the mind ability to see and know, only the intuitive self provide such a Divine gift to be able to see without the mind action.

To be associated with the intuitive self, there is to be a natural expectation to there being no wrong or action to be associated on that Divine level, and to the right of privilege, there is associated an action that is performed by our body life, which is to serve to the greater good of us all.

There is a Mind action that occurs which indicate an action of the Mind that is performing in the density of a profane created mental environment, performed in by our body life and such an environment is not expedient to develop the gift of clairvoyance.

In the Mind where Divine Spirituality is performed, there is no need to make claim to what is to be considered to be a Right or Wrong in the action of our Body Life, remember in Divinity there is where evil does not reside.

Therefore, there is no need to divide the body life action into categories of right and wrong, because in the density of the Divine Mind action, all action is occurring in a relationship that is in Harmony, Order, And balance, meaning in a body life that create a Divine environment, the status quo is Divine body Life living, a Dimension where there is no need to make claim to a right, in order to defeat a wrong.

Those type of classification described categories, are no more than a creation by a Human Being with a Profane Mind, such is not to be found in a Divine Spiritual Environment, which is the natural production revealed by the Divine Mind.

It is a Divine Mind action that acknowledge that which is Divinely True and Real, the two being of the span of space that is eternal and is of endless infinity, only in the density of Time, where all things are taught to be believed about, is such teaching is performed by the profanity of a Human Being Mind.

Divine Energy is used by all things living, the very source that cause the body life to have a mind expression that is not to be associated to the Mind performance, which is why there come with the body life the mental ability to Choose and has the power of Will.

The Divine Energy just provide the body life with such an ability and does not serve as an influence to the body life experiences, which is based upon the quality of your Will and Choice, which is to be decided over the course of our Body Life experiences, yet such become an option to the body life only when that life no longer is performing in the density of its Divine Dimension .

Divine Spirituality assure Divine Thinking and Divine Thinking is revealed by the action of a Divine Mind and when such be the performance by the body life, religious belief is not required nor is capable to be entertained.

So Time is what frame the performance of our body life experiences today, religion once again has served its usefulness as have been created by the Human Beings and now today in the turned frame of the Universe, which put us into frames of dispensation of Time and such Time provide the opportunity to experience Divine enlightenment again.

That Divine Time is what cause religion to become obsolete and irrelevant in the present of the Time of Divine Spirituality which is performed by the body life, causing you to become no longer Human Beings but to become Divine Beings once again.

Your divinity cause you to be as you were before the coming of profane teaching and you transforming into becoming Human Beings, so as you were before so shall you become again, which is Divine Beings, functioning in your Divine Mind, which require no right or wrong, just Divine Living.

Time is Motion and Motion is Eternally Infinite, and infinity is Divine, so Time is not to be considered a possession by the body life, to be used as if to be a currency owned by you.

Such is not the case with Time and you, so the body life is equipped with a Mind of Divine status that fully understand its relationship to Time, which is life in motion, with a body Mind that is of Space, Time, Continuum, meaning it being the sum total of Time that is to be acknowledged in the use of Time and not in the possession of Time.

Time is not to be used as if it is life property and you are to claim ownership of it, the Mind is not to be abused, only to be used to acknowledge the divinity of Time and its relationship to the body life experiences and must be done in a Divine way of thinking, it being an action of the mind that should be performed in Harmony, Order, and Balance, by the body Life action, showing to be the action of a Divine Being.

A Divine Life live its life based upon remembrance and not vain speculation, because all that your body life need to know is already recorded in your Divine Mind body life DNA.

So, when we communicate to teach you the esoteric of life, such information is about that which you already know, you just need to be made to remember what you have been made to forget and that is what religion set out to prevent you from knowing about your body life self experiences.

The Mind is a Universal Vault where all Divine information is residing, profanity is a creation of action by a Mind that is an imitation of the Divine mind and that imitation mind is about having you to be with evil intention, to be acted out in your body life, which become a part of your life experiences, you must come to know that everything that effect the body life, flow through the Mind, be it Divine or profane, in its sifting action.

So to claim to be clairvoyance is to claim the mastery over your Mind self action, which is what play back to you all that is a part of your body life DNA experiences and it is the intuitive self that can show you things that you do not remember, and that is what being clairvoyance is all about.

CHANNELING:

All of these mental experiences take place in the mind of your body life and that is why it is so important that you learn to be in control of your body sense to mind activity.

Now, in order to master the sense to mind action and to be familiar with the power of your mind, then it is possible to send out your mind energy thoughts in such a way it can be effective in affecting others, be they near or far and to channel energy should be for the good of all concern, and not for the evil of it.

Channeling require the Mind to be in a peaceful state, because everything is happening by the mind and you can reach that level of mental discipline in more than one way, but the most common way people make use of it, is by engaging in some kind of ritual that will put the mind at peace, meaning that you be in control of your Mind thoughts, which you are using the mind energy to make the contact with whomever or what ever you are centering your mind energy upon and what for , you have chose to engage your mind to do.

Channeling is transferring energy thoughts to engage other people or animals mind energy thoughts, and it can be done for the good or for the bad, as we say, it require strong concentrated mental focus on the target you have chose to engage, and most Time without the target being aware of it being concentrated upon, that is why it should be done with Divine spiritual intent and not an evil intent, and it take a special mental trained mind, in order to accomplish such a mental act

MEDIUMS:

There are people who claim to be in mental contact with the dead and claim that they are mentally qualified to communicate with the dead and the dead with them, that is called a Mediums, so let us take a look at this claim, which here again, is all taking place in the Mind.

So, is it possible for the dead to speak and is it possible for you to speak with the dead? Well as they say, anything is possible but I say yes you may speak to the dead and no it is not likely that the dead will speak to you, because some things that are claimed to be done is so far fetched, irrational and illogical until it attack profound reasoning and you need those three mental discipline to accomplish being convincing of that which you claim the dead do, which is actual talk, just as the living talk to each other.

Yes, you can speak to the dead, the problem is does the dead talk to you and the answer is no the dead does not, so when there is a claim made about the dead speak, then I SAY TO MAKE SUCH A CLAIM IS DECEIVING.

The only way the dead communicate with you is from the corridor of your mind and not from the grave of their resting place and the Divine energy is not of your life but is for your life to be in your body life form, which give you the ability to speak only when living your body life.

It is a difference in stating an ability to interpret the information that is imbedded in your DNA, which is a deposit of all you are, as a body life Being today, and by being such a life, that is what qualify you to have the ability to enter its chambers and see and hear, as well as know and understand the information coming from your DNA.

The DNA you carry is what represents the myriads of Ancestor generations that cause you to be the embodiment of all of the Ancestors of our past generational lineage, which is what cause you to be the result of your Ancestors.

So it is only in that way, it being our DNA, is the dead able to speak to their living descendant lineage and yet it is such a phenomena that take place in the intuitive self that allow the physical self to mentally connect with the DNA that is our Ancestors of whom we carry, whom we can only hear from in the corridor of our mind action.

Verbally we the living can speak with words or with the use of our mind to the Dead, but the Dead verbally talk not, but with our mind you may communicate with whom ever you so desire, dead or alive.

So it is in that way using the mind, we are all qualified to become mediums that can connect us to our past lives relatives experiences.

The intuitive self action is different from your sense Mind action and it is the intuitive revelation that causes you to know of an occurrence that is a part of your life sequential experiences, past and present.

Such an intuitive revelation that come to you without you using your Mind to activate the revelation that is coming to you, and is doing so inadvertently, many of us refer to such a non-mental generated experience, as being a Spiritual experience, when in fact, it is only the mind that generate a spiritual (attitudinal behavioral) expression from you, with the Mind being the pivotal point of reception of the intuitive revelation coming from the inner ethereal self of your body life.

It is the inner ethereal self that act as the inner mediums that reveal the intuitive information to the Mind of your physical self, and that is what cause you to be able to have mental vision and sudden a experience of nostalgia, that is what it is that will have you to know what you are unable to explain that which you are familiar with, without you having to account for the experience that is being flashed before your sense Mind, to your physical self.

Such a body life phenomena happens without the use of your Mind being the cause of the intuitive action that is coming from your inner ethereal self, and it is that type of body life experience that have you to be recognized as a Mediums that is having an inner Divine Spiritual moment to take place with you in your mind.

The mind is what receive those things that are being revealed to your physical body life, and that is what cause you to have a physical spiritual expressed experience, which cause you to be able to see and reveal things that have happen in the past and is going to happen in the present, before it happen, revealed by the intuitive self.

ASTRAL TRAVELLING:

The Mind is an appalling attribute of the Divine Ethereal Soul entity, it is that none physical entity of the physical body economy, that which give reason to life, the mind can take you places that the physical body life can not go, yet it is the Mind action that reveal the Spirit of the body life action.

The mind can cause your body life to have a Divine experience or it can have your body life to have what we call a bad spirit expression, that which come from a profane experience, everything of the body life expressed by the mind, is coming from the Brain, the information distribution center, it is the mind that give cause for your body life experiences.

The Mind is capable of taking you on journeys that extend beyond the physical body life mobility and ability to take you places that is on the physical level, the Mind can travel beyond the life body physical ability and take you on an astrological journey, traveling throughout the physical universe and into the infinite universe, it being the perfect spatial Night, the Eternal Darkness, the dwelling place of the Divine Essence, the mind is capable of such a performance.

The Mind is capable of taking you on a journey to different solar systems in the universe, to different Galaxies, to Stars and Planets, and you do so, while the physical body life remain stationary on this planet Earth.

To be able to perform such a mental fete, require that you be in possession of your Divine Mind, a Mind that is in Harmony, Order, And is well Balance with the inner ethereal self, as well as with the Universe itself, and with all that bind all things together in the physical universe, that entity being the Divine Essence of all things, in and of the Universe of both kind, caused by the Divine Intelligence, the eternal infinite Divine Energy, the maker of us all.

Astral travel require a mental discipline that have you to be in control of your mind thoughts, it require that you be able to clear the mind of thoughts that are of no concern to the mission you have established for your inner self.

So you mentally focus on the journey and point of destination the mind journey is to take, and you project that mental energy to that point, and allow that mental energy to bring into focus where you have directed it to go, allowing the energy of your mind to take you there, such a mental discipline will allow you to know of things that are beyond the presence of the body life happening.

When you are in the act of astral travel, you bring your destination to you, by the energy action of your mind, though you will be out of your body mind action, which is an inter play with the body life senses, the senses play no part in astral travel, such a travel is based upon your ability to perform mentally, an ethereal physical projection.

As I have shared with you, everything happening by the body life, is mind involved, it is the mind that is the center piece to your physical body life, because the Soul that is present in the body life, is what cause the mind to be with intelligence, and with a mind that give you an ability to know about the soul-mind connection, is the quality of mind that give you the ability to astral travel, taking a journey that is limitless in the scope of the mind ability to astral travel.

DREAMS:

Dreams are a mental action and is part of the mind ability to reveal the body life experiences that have taken place in the past as well as in the present life happening, such a mental phenomena take place when the body life is asleep and can happen while awake, so when dreaming take place while you are experiencing an awake sleep, it is call day dreaming and it is the same mental dynamics that is taking place in the mind, because there is where the dreaming is taking place, while the body life is in a sleep mode.

Dreaming give a panorama view of your life through your DNA, revealing life experiences that you remember and do not remember, but the fact those life actions are being revealed to you in your dream state, flowing in your mind while you are in your body life sleep mode, is evidence that we are an extension of our body life DNA ACTION.

When in you are in your dream state, it is the mind freedom at play, freedom of which it mean that your body sense mind is not controlling that mental revealing process, it is an automatic play back of your life present and past connected experiences, all taking place in the Mind, while in your body life sleep mode, in a dream state, being played back on the celluloid of your mind.

It is the Mind that is at the apex of the body life energy flow, it is the topical ethereal center of your body life, while the soul is the Divine Essence of the body life, producing the inner trinity of the energy action, revealing the pyramid structure of your mind action that is causing the body life spiritual expression, the path the soul energy take, flowing from the soul to the brain to the mind, the brain acting as the body life energy distribution center, as it is received from the soul, the energy source of the body life.

Dreams can inform and edify you and dreams can condemn and convict you.

VISION:

There is a saying that the older we become the more we dream and the dreamer we become, and there is a saying also that says the young among us have visions about our life experiences, past and present, so it is our obligation to bring harmony between the two mental action.

So during the day they say that the young among us are visionaries with much idle Time, which is the reason that the young is able to envision life that has gone by and life that is now happening, having envisioned themselves to become the life they have vision of themselves living in the days past, and in the day that is now.

So the days that are a part of our past and the day that is our present, and within those two dispensation of Time is what the young has vision of, which cause the young to have imaginary visions about the things that they are having an imagination about.

It is the youth with a mind full with past lives experiences and is visualizing about a life they wish to live now, and days to come, as each day of their youthful life provide them the opportunity to write upon the tablet of the youthful mind the action that is now taking place in the youth visionary life.

The days gone by and days now is, such is what cause the young to have visions based upon their desire, and what is desired today, is what the young have visions about what happened yesterday, as the old continue to dream about what did happen in life past, and can be of life experience today, and the young can have visions about what can happen in their lives about things that is a part of out past and present life experiences.

Therefore, without great life expectation and responsibility coming from the young amongst us, it is common for the young to take advantage of what is considered to be idle Time of the young, which is why they have time to be visionary about what could be in the young people lives today.

Some people call the young people who are having visions about what is to happen in their lives, as being day dreaming.

So the old as well as the young, establish a spirit about life that reflect our lives past experiences and how we desire our lives to be in present days experiences and that is how we like for those days that have yet to come, to be.

All things that are happening, is as we desire it to be in our lives and our reaction to those things, first had to have happened in our mind, so all we do in life, involves our mind in such a way, until life action will be in such a way that it will be to our lives advantage or disadvantage, regardless of whether we envision it or dream how our lives have been, or is to be, and how the young envision their lives to be today, start in the young mind.

It is the mind that see farthest those things that have been in our lives and the things that is happening in our lives are the things we desire to have happen in our lives, the mind is what determine our reality, so how we see things become important in how we will cause those things to be, and will have an effect in our lives.

The vision we have about life, is depended upon the way our mind picture them to be, as if to verify, that all things pertaining to our lives, is of the action that is being created by our mind.

Meditation

Chapter 8

GETTING TO KNOW YOU:

You can not understand the things that are happening in and around your lives, not until you are in the know about your life and the best method to engage your self in, so that you can gain knowledge about your self, is the method of meditation.

Meditation is no more of a method than that which enable you to use the mind to bring harmony, order, and balance to your body rhythm and to your thinking ability, meditation being a method that all kind of advice has been given about how to engage in such a mind elevating experience.

Many people of the so call meditation spiritual sect, advise to be used, certain type of rituals in order to perform the act of meditation but I do not, I do not speak against the use of rituals for the purpose of helping you to enter into a meditative state, it is for you to decide what settle your mind.

The ritual use is suggested because meditation require complete mind discipline, like I share with you, the mind is what define your life reality, in and beyond life dimension.

So it is important for you that Divine meditation be the method to use in order to take you beyond into the nonphysical dimension, instead of religious meditation, and there is a difference and the difference is concentration without having a religious predisposition about that which you are concentrating upon.

So first allow me to deal briefly with religious meditation, it is a method used that has Jesus as your center piece, so that you may concentrate upon and to have faith that you will be able to accomplish the goal that is required, before you are able to enter into a ritual of meditation, because the aim and goal is to get God to extend blessings to you and to prepare you to become a better person in order to better serve God.

It is different when entering into Divine meditation, which does not require the use of rituals, even though you may, but the main focus when entering Divine meditation is in getting control of your thought processes, meaning getting in control of your mind, and in Divine meditation, the inner self is your center of concentration and you Divinely meditate not to get God blessing but to get to know you, in order to get to know the Divine Essence (God) and to get to know the habit and spirit of the universe, both of them.

The only way to gain such Divine knowledge about you, which will put your self in a Divine mental position to know about those other happening, is to first bring harmony, order, and balance to the way you reasonable think about all things.

So it is the mind that must function Divinely in order for your body life living to become Divinely Spiritual, your concentration must be in Divine order, it must be in harmony with each mental breath you use and there must be a balance between the outer and inner self of your Being.

You must be able to reach such a mental bliss, in order for you to be able to enter into a Divine trance like state, which all has to do with you controlling the thoughts that emanate out from what is referred to as the mind, because divine meditation is to take you out of your body mind thought process and into the intuitive real of your inner self.   .

So Divine meditation can be in process either when in a physical ritual use, or when you are in a mental ritual useful state of concentration, it can be done by creating for your self a desired atmosphere for physical ritual sake, or it can be done in spontaneous mental concentration, without the need to establish the need for a physical ritual atmosphere.

Such an atmosphere is established by burning candles, having water running softly, music sounding softly in the area where the ritual is taking place, and all else of what ever you need that will put you in touch with your inner ethereal self, the self that will reveal to you the ethereal world that is residing beyond the physical self within the ethereal self.

Yet the main objective is to put you out from the sense mind stage of your outer self and to put you in contact with the inner ethereal self, and when that happen, that is what send you away from the launching pad, your mind, and into the intuitive dimension of your inner ethereal self and that is where you will experience the intuitive spirituality of your inner ethereal self, which will reveal to you things that are not capable of being looked at by the outer self of your Body life Being.

Divine meditation is about putting you in contact with your Divine ethereal self, which will reveal to you knowledge about the ethereal inertness of all there is to know about thyself life, and about the self of existence, which is the universal embodiment of eternal infinity, the perfect night, the Dark essence of your Divine spirituality.

Divine Meditation is not about hearing angels singing or looking for the proverbial white light, or seeking

Jesus, none of those religious symbolic claims, Divine Meditation is about gaining control of your mind thoughts and to be able to direct that soul to brain to mind energy in such a way that it will enhance your Divine spirituality, and the way to do that, is by having control over your mind thoughts.

Meditation divinely, is to put you out of the vicinity of your mind thoughts, which will put you into your intuitive non-mental dimension that is what the Divine out of body experience, really is all about.

Meditation when entered into divinely, can transform you into becoming a very powerful force among the world body lives, qualifying you to be able to repel the evil that is directed against you in the world, yet many, if not most of us Beings, do not use the method of meditation, divinely and wisely.

HEART RHYTHM MEDITATION:

Heart rhythm meditation is about a concentration with alertness that will put your Mind thoughts in rhythm with the heart beat of your Body life, what you are doing by using this method of meditation, is to put your mind thought in harmony with your body vibration, which is coming from the rhythmic beat of the body heart; remember, everything about you, is about the Mind, nothing get pass the Mind on the physical dimension of life activity.

So, when attempting any type of meditation, whether it is heart rhythmic meditation or ritual meditation or spontaneous meditation, all require focus of the Mind, because it is an inward journey that begins with the Mind in control of your mind travel.

When your spirit is of a Divine setting, your spirit being your attitude and behavior, then both of yourselves, body and mind become in such Divine Harmony until there is no limit to what you will become qualified to do, or the degree of subconscious dimension you will be qualified to enter, be it on a mind conscious fantasy illus ional level, which become your body life action become your physical reality or in the mental subconscious level , all such action is of the Mind ability to send you on such a travel that take place in the mind.

It is the mind that does the verifying of the illusion concerning your body life reality and / or your created fantasy.

There is an outer self dimensions which the mind can take you, and there are deeper dimensions that the mind no longer plays a part in revealing to you, that which is happenings on the much deeper out of body life, self dimension, it being the nonphysical revealed world, which is revealed to you, only by the soul within you.

Heart meditation is what require the greater focus and concentration of all, because such a challenge, is based on the equilibrium of the body sense to mind interaction, and the vibration that is emanating from the rhythm of the heart beat, is what give you that sensation coming from the Heart and mind interaction.

Therefore, you must be able to pick up the magnetic current that is being relayed throughout the body, to the body organs, and yet you must be able to coordinate your mind focus with the electrical current that is flowing from the heart with a rhythmic vibration which come from a heart mind meditative state.

So, only the mind can pick up that electric current and assimilate with it, the mind being energy as well, which then qualify the mind to be able to become the subconscious level of the mind unconscious action.

All such mental action is taking place in the mind of your body life, which is where Divine Truth and Reality reside, and can be experienced, and it is in the environment of Divine Truth and Reality.

There is where the Divine spirit is the representative of you, reflecting your mind ability of being capable of obtaining and retaining all information about life experiences, and your life mind is what reveal all that you desire to know, concerning that which pertain to your body life experiences.

Your body life and its mind ethereal existence, such are the jewels of Divine Spirituality, its Divine essence is that which require the mind to be of divine discipline.

Such a mental discipline is in order to be able to experience and verify your Divine Spirituality, and such a dynamic happening that is going on in the physical as well as the Mental dimension, serve to the advantage of living a Divine Life.

Such a life is what have a dimension that cause you to have a certain type of spirit that is divine and that is what reveal the quality of a mental status that you reveal about your self, which is demonstrated by the body life and is revealed by the mind spirit of the body life as well, meaning, the spirit (attitudinal behavior) you display in life, will be either divine or profane.

Heart rhythmic meditation is about listening to the rhythmic beat of your organic heart and by you engaging by listening to the harmonic sound that come from every heart beat and breath and think using that rhythmic sound, it will cause you to be mentally and divinely qualified to interact with the vibrating harmonic of each heart beat that will send you into such a deep subconscious state until you will become aware of the intermediate world that is within your body life self.

It is the mental world that is revealing to you those events that is a part of your past life experiences, as well as your present day experiences, all capable of happening while in your Divine Meditative state, you being guided by the heart rhythmic beat, as it is being recorded by your mind subconscious state, which is between the physical and ethereal dimension of your body and inner life self, we call it the subconscious state of our mind action

APPLIED MEDITATION BY THE MIND:

Applied meditation is about you having the ability to take the mind into an inactive state and that is why you begin by consciously applying methods that will help you exit the conscious and enter the subconscious state of your mind with you being in control of your sense mind activity that allow you to look at and observe the things that are happening in you body life, things that are coming from the exoteric activity of your mind action, while in the conscious mind state of your body life living.

Again, I can not say enough and it can not be overly emphasized enough, about all that you do that is of the physical body life level and it is done by your body sense mind action.

So even when you are attempting to enter into a meditative state, you must apply your self and prepare your self in an effort to enter into that meditative state that will take you out of the sense mind experience and into the subconscious dimension of your mind action.

The fact that meditation is about putting you in an out of mind conscious and into a subconscious state, yet while in a meditative state you are made aware of that which you have preprogrammed your mind to see and to do.

While in your meditative state, you have no control over what you will see, but you can be effective in accomplishing what you have preprogrammed your mind to do, which is to allow you to know about those life experiences, both past and present that is a part of you.

Yes, you can have an effect on that which you have preprogrammed your mind to do, while in your meditative trance.

Applied meditation is all about going into such a mind awareness, and when entered into the subconscious meditative state, which cause you to be without a conscious mind awareness, you will have no control over what you see of the events that are happening on the subconscious level.

So when you go into meditation about that you desire to become aware of, or over what you have preprogrammed your mind to accomplish, such an experience will have an effect in your conscious sense mind life activity.

Meditation, whether it is based on rhythmic heart beat or ritual applied meditation, it can give you an experience that will be a great euphoric comfort, or it can be a dangerous chaotic discomfort when not entering a state of meditation with a Divine Mind, a mind that function in Harmony, Order, And Balance that will cause your meditation experience to be a divine experience.

There is so much advice given on how to meditate, when to meditate, and what type of an environment that is appropriate for meditation, all which is good, but is not necessarily required, in order to enter into a Divine meditative state.

Because, when operating in your Divine Mind, there is no requirement to enter into a meditative state out of the conscious mind and to go into the subconscious state that is not govern by the body conscious mind life action.

It is a Divine Mind that qualifies you to become a Divine Being, because it is the Mind that determines the quality of life you will live and it is the Divine Mind that makes manifest a Divine spirit.

So our Divine spirituality is a reflection of our Divine Mind in action, displaying our body life performance, so applied meditation, it is about putting the conscious mind into a subconscious mind state of action, which is the mind lingering between mind awareness and intuitive revelation.

Controlling the mind is what give you the ability to enter into deep meditation and the deeper your meditation takes you, the deeper you will be in the deeper awareness of the esoteric happenings while in your subconscious state.

The things that will be happening while in your subconscious state, will be the things happening and is being revealed to you while in your meditative subconscious mind state, which is what cause you to be able to see things that you do not normally look at in your conscious sensual state of mind.

SOUL:

Just as the Heart, much has been said about the soul of your body life and it all is based on religious speculation, no facts, just what you are told by those who created the fantasy of religion and all of its parts, with the greatest part being about the soul of your life.

So what I will share in this book about the soul, carry just as much weight as what the creators of your religion tells you about the soul.

The soul is not a physical material entity, it is not matter that can be looked at and touched, yet it is the action that has no beginning or ending, no alternating value in your life.

The soul does not come and then go, such a process of motion is associated to all things that are physical, which are things that can be looked at and touched, such is not the form of the soul.

Life depend on the soul but the soul does not depend on life, it is the body life that has its place in the process of living, because of the soul, and not the soul having its action of existence because of the body life.

It is the soul that is the center of your physical body and provides life to the body physical, which has the responsibility and is given the opportunity to make decisions for your body life.

The soul give the body life the opportunity To Be, and with a sure coming of Time, when life will Not Be.

So the soul is the major representative of your body life, a part of the body life economy that is not physically organic, such as the brain, heart, lungs, kidney, liver, intestines and all of the other body organs, no, the soul is not a part of those body parts, it is the reason those body organs are able to function as a part of the body economy.

There has been given many description of the soul, so when in the act of expressing your sense mind body feelings, one such expression, is when we state to some one that you love that body life of some one, and do so with all of your heart and your soul.

We say thing without thinking about what we are saying, we just express our feelings based on what we believe about what somebody has told us to believe about ourselves.

So with our soul, we believe we can love with it as well as hate with it, and in our life living, we are told that we have a need to save the soul, as if it is in danger in our body life, and it has been disobedient to a religious God, which make it to become punishable by God.

I must say, such a belief about the soul will keep you from experiencing your Divine Spirituality, which is the action that can cause Joy, Peace, and the Greater Good in your body life, for you to experience.

The Soul is a member of the ethereal organs expressed by the body life, those organs are non-physical and can not be looked at, nor can they be touched, they are intangible entities that are important to the body life ability to be expressive, while your body life live, and life mean to be in action and to be observable mobile.

The Soul is the master ethereal organ to your body life and there is nothing about your body life that supersede the soul, and there is the Mind and Spirit, all consist of the ethereal organs of the body life that is not physical.

There is much talk in the spiritualist community about the Pineal Gland, though in the medical field it is claimed to have such a gland but have not been able to extract such a Gland.

Never has a Pineal Gland ever been surgically removed from the body life, yet there is the claim of such a Gland being a part of the body life economy.

It is my contention that the Soul and the Pineal Gland is the one and same ethereal organ in the body, all ethereal organs are not attached to the physical body life, they are in the body but is not a part of the physical body organic attachment, such as the soul, Mind, and Spirit, is not, these are entities of expression and not physical function, which is what the body life organs are required to do.

So the question no doubt that your mind is asking, what is the Soul, well it is an entity that is present inside and outside and around our body, causing it to be alive and functioning, it is the Divine Energy that is the Essence of the body and give cause for life to be of the body .

The Soul as I have shared with you to be the center, the central theme of your body life and without it, the body life cease to be, it is the death that is connected to life and the life that is connected to death, without it there is no life.

So the Soul is the Divine essence to your body life, it is the source that provide all of the body life energy that is needed to sustain the body life and its ability to function expressively, meaning that all about the body life is no more than Energy.

So the soul is Divine Energy, and that energy is mere intelligence, which is why the body life economy is to function in Harmony, Order, And in Balance with each other, with the brain directing the organic function of the body life.

There is only one Soul that cause myriads of functions in the body life, and to the body life, it function as the body mind, and spirit, with the spirit of the soul being the final act of the soul function, as is displayed by the body life, revealing its expressed action as the spirit of the body life, which is the expressed display of the body attitudinal behavior, it being the physical expression by the body life.

It is the soul that does not attempt to interfere with the body life, in the way it express itself, the Soul neither influence nor encourage the body life, it provide the body life with the intelligence to have a Will and to make choices based on the function of the body economy, which consist of the body senses and the body mind and its attributes,

It is the mind ability to think and reason, and since the spirit is the expression of the body life, it is the Soul that gives the mind authority over the self of the body life.

The soul is the center piece, the generator of life, it is what provide life having all of its intentions, one which is to get to know the body self.

So in order to know thyself, you must be in complete acquaintance with the mind capability, because only through the mind, do all information flow.

 Information about the past lives of which you are attached to, and the present life you are getting to know about, be it in the exoteric of your body life experience or in the esoteric ethereal dimension of your mind action, which reveal the state and the quality of your soul generated spirituality.

It is not the soul that is in need of our attention, it is our mind and the quality thereof that cause and determine the quality of our body life, which we will live, and the more in control of your spirituality, the more we will be qualified to interpret and use the information that flow to the mind from our soul.

The soul provide our mind with the ability not to have the want to believe but with the ability to know about all that had happen to the lives we are a part of and the life we are being in the experience of in our present life Time.

We should receive all thoughts about our lives that come to us from the soul to the mind and learn from them, the soul which is informing us about the myriads of yesterdays that our lives have experienced and all thoughts that are of our present life experience that is guiding our lives today.

We are required to take no thought for tomorrow, leaving the tomorrows to eventually become today, while we must do all we can to make tomorrow to become the best today we can, for our body life to live and experience in our lives, not tomorrow, but today.

It is the responsibility of your mental spirituality to demonstrate your body life action, so as your spirit is revealed by the action of your Mind, then your mind is what make it to be so highly important when attempting to obtain through expression, your Divine Spirituality.

So it is important for you to know the action of the soul and the performance of the Mind and how the two are related to the brain action, because the quality of life that is to be lived Divinely, require that your Mind must be of Divine quality before you can be able to experience your Divine Spirituality, that which is reflected by your attitudinal behavior which is demonstrated by your body life action.

I do desire that you do understand, that which you are reading in this book about the body, soul, mind, heart, spirit, and all else that this book is revealing about your Divine Spirituality.

The Soul (Divine Energy) Is The Divine Essence (God) To Your Body Life

EMOTION:

Emotion is an act that display an expression of the body sense mind, and we have come to identify and define such a sense mind expression, using various terms such as Love, Hate, Happiness, anger, Sad, fear, and Joyful, to name a few.

We feel as if those terms better describe our body action of emotion, which is no more than a vivid indication of how the sense mind is capable of displaying the body life action that is demonstrated in a very demonstrable way using physical expression.

We label our emotions in order to indicate the level and quality of the sense mind we are functioning with, which become an indication of how we describe our feelings, which is no more than an expression of our mind thoughts in a dramatic and / or mild display of passion, expressed toward someone or something.

Emotion is a vivid display of how someone is thinking of and about someone or something, that is what we call feelings, which are acted out in an emotional way, be it in dramatic fashion or in a mild and calm fashion.

Either way, it is an indication of someone thinking about you and it describe the intensity of those thoughts and those thoughts have everything to do with how you classify your life expressed emotions, as we label them to be right or wrong.

Emotion is just an expression of the mind thoughts displayed by the body action, sometime controllable and sometime it is not, which can bring a feeling of security and protection or a felling of fear and destruction.

All emotions are done by a display of your body life spirit, which can be a divine emotional display of your spirit (attitudinal behavior) or a profane display of your spirit, it is about the quality of your emotion (mind) that describe and give it a value that is acceptable to your body life or is unacceptable to your body life.

We express ourselves in a very different emotional way, causing our lives to be of high intense drama and of a calm intense expression, all being depended on how we have the mind to cause our body to react to what our sense of perception is looking at or what our mind has the ability to see, which can have an affect upon the body life, such is referred to as a mental and physical display of our emotions.

Emotion reveals the state of our mind, which can serve for the better or for the worse in the way our body follow the guidance of our mind, which display the quality of our spirit.

CONSCIOUS:

Conscious is an awareness of the mind energy that display thoughts that are made known by the quality of spirit the mind display and the body reflect, revealing the body life in the way it is acting and reacting, in response those events that affect our lives.

Conscious is what cause an awareness of those things that are involved in our lives and do surround our lives, because all things happening and is effecting our lives, can cause our mind to have our body to act and react in such a way that reveal us to be cognizant of the things effecting our lives.

Those things can cause our conscious to be no more than an awareness of those things the mind instruct us to be aware of, and do assign value to all things that appear on the physical level of our lives, which has an effect upon our lives and determine how we act and react to any apparent situation that is effecting our lives.

It is not commonly mention that the Universe has a conscious, indicating that the universe is aware of its surroundings and all that is a member of it, and is affected by its action.

so if the Universe has a conscious, it can only mean that conscious is no more than Energy and energy is intelligence with a conscious that has the power to guide and direct all things, but do not influence the action of those things that is displayed by the bodies that consist of the Universe.

Only physical things influence other physical things, because the not physical, has no need to influence, it is the energy that give the body of things the power of influence and the ability to repel as well as attract each other.

So the conscious of the universe is the energy that cause the universe to be alive and life is motion, so it is from the motion of the universe that energy is extended one to the other of its physical bodies, causing each to be conscious of the other, verifying that all things that is a member of the physical universe as well as the nonphysical universe.

So all of those things that are physical and nonphysical, they happen to be connected to each other, thus you have what is referred to, in regard to the universe, it having a binary systematic relationship with all parts that constitute the universe and is bounded by the universe conscious, we knowing that it is the Energy that bind and it being the intelligent conscious that cause the universe to be aware of all of its parts.

So, as the Universe move around into different window position, the Energy change in intensity and the higher the energy frequency is, the more conscious elevated the universe bodies become and is increasing the level of energy that the body come to experience, that is what increase the energy flow which elevate the body mind.

The mind it is, that is deeply penetrating into the various mental dimensions, causing an intense elevated awareness(conscious) of all things that are of the past and all things now is in the present, and all things that is to come and is beyond the mind being capable to go.

It is the intuitive ethereal state of your out of body existence that become your informed reveler of the action that is of and within the Divine Darkness, the place where there reside the Divine Essence, it being the Infinite and Eternal Intelligence to all things that are and are not in physical form.

SUBCONSIOUS:

This level of consciousness serve to be the Mind last stage of conscious awareness, which is not generated at the mind level of your body life action, this is the stage of awareness that the conscious mind did not pick up during the time of your sense to mind interaction, some people refer to such a happening as being a subliminal not conscious awareness.

Yet, such life happening is recorded by the Mind action but is by passed by the conscious recorded awareness, and those

Unconscious events that took place in your life, they are stored in a esoteric compartment in your mind and is played back to make you aware of their presence.

It is done without the mind conscious level action, the part of the mind that did not play a part in such a conscious recording, which is why the subconscious level of your mind action is not of your mind conscious awareness.

The subconscious of your mind action serve as the archive to your subliminal recorded happenings and much that have happen in your life is stored there in the subconscious, which is not of your ability to imagine.

Such require a mental method as meditation to serve as the mental key in order to enter the archive of your subconscious library and there in the mind, are your subconscious recorded life happenings.

It is the subconscious that is the disconnect from the conscious level of your sense to mind action, it is the conscious mind that reveal the happenings that you are aware of.

It is your body sense to mind that causes all of the illusion reality the sense has caused your mind to record and label, in order to be your reality and truth, and that is all that the body life is functioning by.

Your sense to mind is the action that causes you to be able to determine your sense of reality, which is an established illusion, all taking place on the physical level for the purpose and benefit of your body life.

It is the sense to mind that is responsible for your level of conscious or subconscious experience, and that is what gives your body life meaning.

You can live your life in an illusion of physical reality, you being reminded of your past lives, of which you are a part of, and it is your present life you live, even though you are a part of someone else past lives, as well as the life you are presently living today.

Yes, it is the mind conscious and subconscious state that is aware and is unaware of the mind action that take you through the dimension door way that leads into Divine truth and Reality, the dimension that is not of a conscious state, but is of your intuitive revealing state, a level and action beyond the mind state of conscious.

Subconscious is an action that is in a state of out of mind action, it is there where into the ethereal divine dark space of eternal infinity, a Divine inert action is in an ethereal state of eternal motion, in a state of existence.

The subconscious, which is made to be known, not by the mind action but by the alchemic intuitive action that is happening in a dimension from where Divine Truth and Reality is revealed to you and everything that is To Be, and is as if things are Not, and yet, it all is as the Divine Essence produces all things To Be.

Start Here

So in order for you to see and comprehend all that is and all that seem not to be, it require a Divine Spiritual intuitiveness to reveal such a Divine Reality to you, in order for you to be able to know and understand without conscious and subconscious comprehension.

Divine Reality is of the Divine Essence (GOD) and all things that happen in and beyond your body life, is being caused in your body life because of the Divine Energy connection that all life has to the universe.

The intuitive action is a frequency of energy in the body that is separate from the mental energy activity that inform as well as guide your body life, which is on a frequency where the body life mind can be in a conscious and subconscious state of awareness, and such an awareness is of the happenings that is played back to you in various body life performances.

The Mind consciously and subconsciously is reminding you that all of those lives performances which the mind is qualified to remind you of, is of your life past performances, that is coming from your mental action, and is displayed right before you, on an ethereal dimensional level that is of your mind, and beyond your mind.

That is what reveal that the mind has recorded all of your body life activities, even to the point of serving as a mean that lead to the body life conscious, that either condemn you for performing certain types of body life activities, or could it be the conscious that cause you to be of confidence with approval, in the way you are performing in those body life conscious and subconscious activities.

All of the body life activities are being displayed by the expression of your body life spirituality. (Attitudinal behavioral action)

All life with a level of intelligence, is of a mental conscious and subconscious awareness, of all that life is and has been engaged in on the body life physical level of that life living Being.

EGO, ENVY, JEALOUSY:

EGO:

I REFER TO THE VANITY OF EGO, ENVY, JEALOUSY, AS THE TRINITY OF EVIL; I WILL BRIEFLY ADDRESS EACH INDIVIDUALLY.

I will begin with ego a vainly expressed personality with a conscious that is without condemnation of such a life spiritual expression, a life that is self centered and elevated to be more than what it is pretending to be.

The body life with a vain ego is highly depended upon the sense aspect of that body life and being overly sensitive can work to the detriment of that life expressed personality, which is a spirit of self induced involvement to the point of always wanting to be the center of attraction, even at the cost of injury, lying, and deceit to others.

To be vainly egotistical which violate the threshold of self confidence in your own ability to accomplish that which you strive for in life, even to the point you are never satisfied to be able to applaud the accomplishment of others.

Even when those others want to feel being the most important in what ever group or individual endeavor you might become engaged in with others, and it all being a play of the mind, and it being at the mind of the matter of your spiritual exposure, vain and profane it is.

Vain ego can cause you to kill or to be killed, it is as a cancerous virus of the mind without a conscious that condemn.

To express a vain ego prevents you from being able to express a Divine spirit, a spirit of expression that is of divine attitude and behavior toward your corresponding Beings, commonly expressed as your fellow mankind, female and male you are.

Vanity in the expression of your ego is an expression of evil,

Such a profane vain ego expression does not take into the consideration of the sensitivity and respect of others.

ENVY:

Envy is another vain and profane personality of evil expression, an act of the body life that prevents you from being able to experience your Divine Spirituality, when being in such a vain envy state of mind.

To be envious, is always being in a wanting state of mind, wanting what others have that you do not have and hate the fact that someone have what you want, and need I say, that such is a vile and vain spirit to have to be a part of your self.

Just as there is Divine and profane vain ego, so is there profane vain envy and it is the profane vain expressed personality that hinders the ability to express your Divine Spirituality.

To be of dislike and of hate of others because others may have what you want, but do not have, it will cause you to move to try and demean those for having what you do not have and want.

Many people have what they have from decent and hard work, that is what cause you to have such an evil display of spirit that reveal your character and personality toward them.

There is no association with Divine Spirituality by you, when you are expressing your self in such a way, a spiritual expression of peace is when you are able to be in harmony, order, and balance with your self, revealing a higher quality of mental conscious, where the evil of envy can not reside.

JEALOUSY:

Here is an expressed personality that is closely related with envy, even though it is the ego that is the root cause of the profane vain expression of such a evil personality spirit, in an action displaying a vain ego, envy, and jealous personality.

It is jealousy that breeds anger over the fact that someone is in possession of something you can not and do not have, it just tears you apart mentally and personality wise.

So, to see someone in Divine spirit and appear to have their life in Divine order to the point it change the outward appearance when expressing such a Divine spirit, while it is causing your beautiful personality to shine with such a radiant glow, indicating that you are in possession of the greater good of your self.

Being in a Divine state of mind and state of conscious, that will allow you to express your Divine Spirituality, something that profane vain jealousy will not allow you to experience in your body life, that is what being in Divine order is all about.

Jealousy like envy, is attached to the root of evil, it being the vanity of ego, and it is the practice of jealousy that can cause you to become spiritually insane.

With jealousy, you are no longer in control of your mind thoughts and you are expressing a spirituality that is evil and vainly profane, it being the act of somebody whose body life action is not the expression of harmony, order, and balance with the life action of the universe.

The universe is the Master Teacher of Divinity to all members of the Universe that desire to function in their body life, in a Divine Spiritual way of expression, one that reveal the state that your mind is functioning in.

1. LOVE:

Allow me to deal with the emotion we refer to as Love, so what is love other than a vivid description of our mind thoughts that generate an action by our body life that is demonstrated in such a way it bring a comfort of mind that give you a euphoria high.

Love is most time, indescribable, and can become of such high intensity until if it is not received by the person it is being directed toward and that person indicating a return of that loving affection, it can cause the person displaying that quality of emotion in the fashion of love, to turn that love into a fury of rage with such intensity, until it can cause body harm to the one shown such a high quality of love toward you.

So love can start out to be a Good display of emotion and can end up becoming a very destructible act of emotion, it being done in the name of that emotion we call love.

Love is an act of our mind thoughts that is being expressed toward the one told to be loved, yet love is not always calm, submissive and kind.

Love can be of an aggressive hostile emotion, coming from the person doing the loving, displaying an emotion that will cause harm to the one being told is loved, and that type of emotional act is claimed to be done, in the act of love.

There is so much that is said about the emotion , love, it is said without the use of thought, it is just based on the emotion of feeling, which can only come based upon the sense mind action, and the thing that give divine quality to that love emotion, is not based upon what you are able to look at, alone, but is based upon what you think about of that you see in its entirety.

So all of love emotion is being played outwardly by your mind, so what is love? It is mind thought and not sense mind perception, even though thoughts are generated by that process, it is the mind that verify love, and the quality of that love, is determine by the quality of your mind.

If your mind is divine, then your love is divine, other wise, you are operating on the profane level with a profane mind, love coming from the interaction of your sense mind action that become the main product that guide your body life spirit.

The spirit being the exoteric expression of your attitudinal behavior, a level of expression that can reveal acts of deceit and confusion, which is operating in a state of illusion and is calling such a profane state of all you are looking at, to be reality that is revealed by the profane sense of your body life action.

It is the sense mind action that is controlling that loving level of your body life performance, a level where love either is or is not trustworthy.

Love being expressed by your sense mind body expression, displayed by a spirit revealed by your attitudinal behavior, a sense mind perceived thought action, is not all the Time expressed as we so desire it to be expressed in our at of loving expression.

You hear people saying such a thing about love, in an effort to define love, such as, God Is Love, yet they are not qualified to define God, yet you claim that you can define Love by associating it to God, as if God is one that express emotion.

God is not a God of emotion, therefore it is not a God of love, God the Divine Essence, It Is A God Of Action, the Divine Essence is that which enable us to do all that we do, but is not the director over all that we do.

It is our action that is based upon our Mind thoughts alone, because God is not an action that dictate, but is an action that generate the energy you need to be alive.

God is the Producer of your Body Life and not the actor of your life, it is only you who carry that sole responsibility for your own emotion, as well as all of those other attributes that is contributed to your body life action, which is based upon your freedom of Will, and Choice, in your Life.

Love is just an emotion that expresses the temperament you have in life, and your ability to reveal such an emotion, that will compliment your life and the life of others in a Divine way, and not a profane selfish egotistical way.

So by the need of Divine expression of our Love for each other, we all should be striving to be able to express our Divine Spirituality, because without it, we can not have the ability to express divine Love for each other, and such an ability to express such a quality of love, is what give you the ability to express your love for the Divine Essence. (GOD)

The Divine Essence has no responsibility to us, it is our responsibility we have to ourselves and to be Divinely expressive toward ourselves, and in so being, we become Divinely expressive toward the Divine Essence and all others, and it is done by a show of divine love and respect toward the Divine Essence, love meaning only mind expression.

It is the fact of our Body Life that show the Divine expression of the Divine essence to us, and there is no greater and Higher emotion that can be expressed than the emotion of love for ourselves, and in so doing, we end up displaying such a quality of Divine Emotion we have for the Divine Essence.

The Divine Essence being the reason for us all To Be, we in a body of Life, which we played no part in causing for ourselves, To Be, and will come soon, Not To Be, a process of a continuum that only the Divine Essence is the Authority over, concerning our body life and all of its attributes.

There is an emotion of Divine quality and there is an emotion of profane quality, one elevate the life by the action of Divine self expression and the other debase the life in an act of Profane self expression.

So it is up to you to determine which quality of emotion you choose for your life, and that choice is entirely up to you and not God.

SPIRITUALITY:

Spirituality is one of the most misconceived terms we use today and as long as we approach that term, using a religious base for its relevancy, we will not be able to grasp the Divine relevancy of such a term as Spirituality.

In order to experience your spirituality you need to know and understand the true meaning the mind is to the spirit, and you must know what constitute the spirit, because such knowledge will determine the quality of your spirituality, that which you will express and display by your body life action.

The spirit of your body life is no more than the attitude and behavior that reflect your state of mind, which is demonstrated by your body life action.

The spirit is not some separate ethereal body of your self, floating around in and out side of your body, as religion has conditioned you to believe about the term, spirit.

The spirit, which is associated to your body life, is no more and no less than being your sense mind expression, as so demonstrated by your body life performance and it is the mind that determine the quality of your spirit.

The Mind has all to do with your body life spirituality and the quality of it, be it Divine or profane, all which is taking place in your mind and is being revealed by your attitudinal behavior, so your spirituality is no more than an attitude reflecting the way that you are behaving in life.

You can not enter the esoteric ethereal (spirit) Dimension by displaying a profane spirit, (attitudinal behavior) we must learn how to recalibrate our mind in order to have it to function divinely, when dealing with the body life action.

Everything about life should be about Divinity and not Humanity, because being Divine is esoteric in nature while Humanity is profanely exoteric and is out of nature, each depending on the quality and status of your Mind and not your spirit, because it is the mind that produce the quality of your spirit.

What is most important about life is living it today to its highest caliber of expression, taking no thought about tomorrow but using your thoughts to master today, and learn from today about your yesterdays.

It is your life present Time which is about your life past Time and such knowledge is most important to your life today, because your past lives serve to be a prologue of your present life.

Did I not warn you that this book is not about conforming, but is about helping you to become transformed into becoming the originality of your body life once again?

When one speak against the Spirit you display, is it because we do not know the value of ourselves and the life we have been given to live unconditionally, or is it we just do not know the Divine True Meaning of our Spirituality and what it Truly consist of?

Most Time when we discuss Spirituality, we feel a need for religion to be its caveat for some reason, and the reason is because we have been conditioned so well in the theology of religion, until we now, many Time without us doing so consciously, use religion as our base for whatever the topic of discussion may be, in order to secure our point we are attempting to make.

So it is religion that taints any point we might be attempting to make about any topic we are commenting on or raising a point of position about, especially when the topic is Divine Spirituality.

It is our Spirituality that reveal our life status in this world and it is our spirit that indicate what our thoughts are regarding every aspect of our lives, so to speak ill of your Divine Spirituality is to speak ill of Divine life and it is your life that you have been given the responsibility to protect and serve for your life self, beloved reader.

So, what is the spirit of your life Being, other than your attitudinal behavior, that you display in life, and those life actions are the prime principles of which you are capable of revealing the quality of mind that is guiding your life.

So if your spirit is of such that you do not respect your life to the point you have allowed somebody other than your self to chart the course for your life to live, then you are no more than a believer in the way that have been prescribed for you to live your life.

Such a prescription carry for your life a religious base, meaning that you live your life with the spirit religion has cultivated within your Mind, and it is religion that have so call poor people lives of this world in the condition it is in today, which is a condition not to be desired if you love your life.

Start Here:

So no, we as People of the world should never rise expressing a spirit that is against the life process that is determined by the way you use your Mind to develop and express your Spirituality.

Spirituality can be of a Divine expression or it can be of a profane expression which depend on who it is that is in control of your Mind that will determine the quality of your spirit.

So when you are functioning in your Divine mind it is your Spirituality which a Divine Mind produce and will not allow you to become idle and complacent with your life condition, when it is in a state of misery and suffering, no matter who you are, no matter what your life condition may be.

In your divine mind, you will always be striving for your life to be able to enjoy the greater good that will reveal a Divine spirited expressed life.

Your Spirituality, when it is actively divine, it is the most potent weapon you have in your possession, to use in the act of expressing your self and will also qualify you to know what it is you must do in order to secure for your life with peace and joy.

So, even when you are in a confined state that cause your life misery, you must develop the quality of mind that give you the ability to express your Divine Spirituality, a mind that will be free from the profanity of the world.

Can you understand That, Beloved Reader?

God, Spirt, Motion, Reincarnation: The Divine Essence: (God)

Chapter 9

God, spirit, motion, and reincarnation, these are entities that appear alchemically without a tangible base, yet they hold and do capture the imagination of all who can be a reasonable and rationally thinker, being able to form thoughts that produce a logic about all the things that are thought about in order to reach a consensus about what is true and real concerning that which we label to be the Divine Essence, (God) spirit, motion, and reincarnation.

It is as if intelligence in material life form capable of rational and logical thought is driven to know about and understand the alchemy of the cosmos, which consist of the Divine essence, (God) Spirit, Motion, and a belief in reincarnation of things gone past and to come back again.

Mortal intelligence of Mankind is so driven to understand the alchemy of the Cosmos until we have affixed our own definition, meaning, and labels to the Cosmos, even though we are without the Divine facts to substantiate our claim.

Take the Divine Essence for instance, it being without a nature with a material base, its existence being the Divine Truth and Reality that is verified by its action and that verification being the Cosmos and the ethereal existence that is beyond its physical boarders.

The cosmos, verifying there being two Cosmos, one is of material matter with limits and the other is immaterial, resting in an ethereal inert state of undetectable motion.

Yet, it is THE Divine Essence that is capable in revealing the Divine fact that It truly and really exist, that fact being the Cosmos which need no verification of it being there because of the alchemy of the Divine Essence and It being in such a Divine state of inert existence.

The Divine Essence does not need to be of Material capability in order for you to understand the Dynamic Phenomena of the Existence of its forever existing presence.

So what do we mortal Beings of reasonable intelligence do, well we now attempt to reduce all that we are not in the know of, and is without understanding of, to a level that fit our ability to believe without the knowledge to understand.

We, most of us, use a belief system as our base that cause us to have faith and hope in that we have reduced to our level of belief, a belief system that we hold about those alchemic principles which we do not know nor do we understand, those principles being the Divine Essence, Spirit, Motion, and Reincarnation.

It is the Divine Essence that has caused the Cosmos to be, the cosmos being the elements that are looked at and the elements that are not able to be looked at.

Yet all is there in the cosmos to be seen through the prism of our Divine mind, the Divine Essence being the alchemy and inert ethereal entity that is the cause for the Cosmos to be, having all of its parts to be banded together moving in a relative fashion, each part having an effect upon the other.

The Cosmos, being the Child of the Divine Essence whose resident is the infinite spatial universe, meaning the only one Divine Infinite Perfect Night that encapsulate the physical Cosmos.

The Divine Essence is genderless, yet it has produced things with a gender base, so to reduce the Divine Essence to the level of being a Man or a Woman, reduce the power of the alchemy of the Divine Essence, and all such imagery of the Divine Essence, as has been presented by mortal Beings with reasonable and rational intelligence, is no more than an expressed imagination of their Divine Essence, (GOD) with a physical image in the form of a gender Being.

You know, it seem as if we have some vain egotistical jealousy toward the Divine Essence (God), we acting as if we have a need to be in competition with that which has caused us to be, as we are seemingly always telling Lies About The Divine Essence (God) that is always in eternal infinite existence.

It is the Divine Essence that is solvent, yet all things are insolvent in the presence of the Divine Essence and to know of these things will put you on the path of being able to express your Divine Spirituality.

SPIRIT:

Many people have been led to believe that there is a Spirit entity with a world of its own and that world is capable of being entered into by a spirit entity that we carry inside of us, such a way is not how I TAKE TO THE SPIRIT To Be.

The spirit is not a BEING, in the physical sense as you and I, it is some what different than the established belief is about the Spirit.

Up to now, YOU HAVE BEEN ABLE TO READ IN THIS BOOK and I have shared with you what the spirit is in relationship to the physical Being, which is, the spirit is an expression of an attitudinal behavior and is not an ethereal immaterial entity trapped between a claimed dimension of life and death, or can interact between those claimed dimensions, as many of you have been led to believe all about that which you have been told to believe about the spirit.

It is a common saying that the dead know nothing, but it is my contention and I will share with you what I Think about the dead, which is that the dead know all that the dead has had the opportunity to experience and to know, when the dead was alive, and that the dead speak to you only by mere fact that you are alive and not because the dead is dead.

You are alive carrying the DNA of the dead that is a part of your Body life and whatever action that was done by the dead, is now a part of you and that is what verify that death is only a perceived action and it has nothing to do with a spirit entity, but it does has all to do with a mind expression.

The mind is what has the ability to interact with the Genome (dead) of your Being, which is a part of your body life make up, so the question become, is there a spirit entity that live inside of us and is it the spirit that travel into the various levels of our subconscious dwelling dimensions that is beyond our body life present experiences?

Is it the dead that is a part of us that give us cause to make such an astral journey or to see things that the sense eye can not look at and have us to know things that has happened way beyond our present body life Time experiences?

Need I say that such is not the doing of a so call spirit entity having a form and shape, so I ask, is all such a happening about spirits taking place in the mind activity?

The mind is what reveal the body life spirit expression and without the mind there will be no body life spirit to express, so it is the mind that is of your body life that make manifest your life spirit and it is the quality of that mind that determine the quality of your body life spirit and will determine the degree and depth of your Spirituality.

Your Spirituality must be Divine in order for you to venture beyond the chambers of the subconscious life level of your mind.

The spirit is a part of the body life economy, it is what determine the level, depth, and quality of your life Spirituality, meaning that if your attitude and behavior is of such a Divine Quality then that is what allow you to enter the alchemic world where the esoteric ethereal happenings are taking place and that is what will qualify you to know of things that are happening and have happen in and beyond your body life living in the present and the past Time, the life past Time being beyond the ability of the body life sense of mind to know of those Times.

The spirit world is your out of mind world of esoteric ethereal happening, a world consisting of non physical behavioral action of which its spirit can be revealed to you by what I refer to as intuitive revelation, which is not a part of the body life mental spirit but is a part of a phenomena occurrence of an action that is happening and is revealing things about your past and present lives and did those lives did live at a Time in the past as a part of your body life living experience.

We can bring changes to our body life that is experiencing conflict, disorder, and imbalanced living, by the way we control our mind, and it is the spirit we express that come from the mind action that make those things happen that we are concentrating and focusing our mind upon, in order to cause what we desire to happen to happen.

Everything depend on the quality of your mind which reveal the quality of your spirit and your mind must be of a Divine quality which will make what you desire to happen to be favorable to your body life.

A Divine Mind Spirit is what should be desired and expressed at all Time and it must be the quality of your mental environment that cause you to be able to display your divine spirituality.

A spirituality that will reveal the personality needed to elevate your life living condition or will lower your living standards, all of those things that are happening in your life, good or bad that is happening based upon the quality of your mind thoughts.

So it is not the ritual of the meditative act that put you on the Divine path that lead to the esoteric ethereal dimension of your mind unconscious state.

It is the quality of mind that cause your spirit to be able to become dissolved into the intuitive existence of the inner self and it is there where Divine Truth and Reality reign supreme away from your mind thoughts.

The esoteric action of your intuitive happening is what reveal a Divine awareness, having an ability and desire to act to protect your body life way of living from the profane action that go on in the world.

Your body life protection being depended upon that you functioning in your Divine Spirit that must be a part of your body life way of living.

So what is the cause for all of your mental and spirit happenings?

It is the Divine Essence of your body life that is giving the soul to life, which is the cause for your body life action and the manifestation of your spirit.

The soul is what display your life action and it all is how you cause your life to be that which has happened in the past and present of your body life experience.

It is your spirit (attitudinal behavioral) expressing an awareness that is being revealed by your sense mind, and it is a sprit action that is not a action of your sense mind that is revealed to your body life, but is an action being caused by the soul intuitive happening, that is revealing information coming from your ethereal inner self of the soul, the soul being the Divine Energy that cause life to be.

The spirit you display toward those events that are happening in your life will determine the quality of your life living, so it is the spirit coming from your mind action that cause your body action, and can cause a change to come to your body life condition, if need be.

MOTION:

Motion is a concept of manifest reality, meaning that you can not see motion but you can look at things that we perceive to be in motion and because all things seem to be changing, the conclusion is that all things are in constant motion, so motion is change and change is the verification of life.

Life is an act of motion and you can not see it happening but you do experience the result of that motion that is happening in life and just as we can not see the actual motion that cause the alternation between night and day, we can not see our life motion that bring on the process of what we refer to as aging and that is what cause the change in your body life appearance.

So it is with the mind and the spirit that cause in our lives, us to think and reveal the spiritual action of our thoughts and what ever our spirit reveal through our expression of it, that is what reflect our life condition that is caused by the way that we act and behave in life.

Life is taking place by the sense mind action process that many of us just take for granted and do not realize that we determine the direction our lives are to move through life.

All of your life action is taking place in the motion of our mind action and our body life being the verification of that motion and being that life is motion and motion become the spirit of our life and the way we express the motion activity of our mind become, then it is our mind that cause the expression of our spirituality.

So whether our spirituality is that of Divine quality or profane quality, it is revealed in the way that we act and behave in the motion which is life.

So our attitudinal behavior is what reveal our spirit and guide our motion in life, and the emotion we display in life, that come from the interaction between our sense mind action.

The motion of the mind action is what our spirit is based and on how we express what ever it is that we are thinking about in the motion of our mind body life.

So motion is a spiritual experience and it can take you places in your mind you can not remember to have ever been, but as the saying goes, there is nothing that happen in your life that is new in the presence of the Sun, to paraphrase such an original saying about the happening over the course of our lives.

Motion is the grace and beauty by which life flow and it can be of a spiritual experience that give life a euphoria experience of great satisfaction or it can be of such an action that life experience can be of great dissatisfaction, all taking place through the sense, mind, spirit motion of your life activity.

Divine Spirituality is the ultimate mental orgasm in the action of the sense, mind, spirit, motion interaction that is expressed emotional by us in our life.

REINCARNATION:

There is nothing that is real and factual about the claim of there being an action that cause the life of a Being to be reincarnated after the action of death, that is just a belief fostered by those of religious faith and hope, believing death is not the end all of life.

We have been allowed to experience life by our body life action, so we harbor the belief that life as we have lived it before, come back around for us to live it again, either in our life form we had been given before in our original experience in life or in some other life form, with life maintaining the same life mental attributes of the previous life form in which we lived our lives.

Reincarnation is an irrational stretch of the imagination about life experience and it is an attempt to give life reason and purpose for being and to have a need for a return performance, claiming the same life was once before.

So, if life does not return with the same mind as before, in the same life form as before, then what would be the purpose in returning in a different life form, that is what is causing such a belief to be out of bound of reasonable, rational, logical happening.

Reincarnation is a tenet of religion fantasy, it has no basis of empirical fact to warrant a rational discussion about it, and it only serve as a cloak over the fear of death, which serve as the end chapter for life as we have lived it to be, in our life Time.

Reincarnation is an attempt to exploit the fact that motion present two phases of its action, one is finite in the life of its action and the other is infinite in the existence of its ethereal formless action, one has limit and the other is without limit.

Although in the process by motion, it is a continuous process of actual production of physical things as had been produced before, but with new bodies and with the same form, but it is different from that which had came before.

Even though the performance is of the same task as the other bodies had performed before, with the difference being a new body but same action.

So being a physical corporeal Being, but assessing the same set of circumstances in life differently, is what cause you to not be the Being who once were here before the coming of the new Being, with the two being one and the same in term of being of the same template and blueprint as before.

The decision process of information is different by the new body and that is what make you out to be not the Life body Being that was here before death exit your life body, as life ushered into a new body life Being, coming from a state of nonphysical existence to a formed life physical Being.

It is given life to once live to be, and then not to be, and not to be is to exist Divine, infinitely, eliminating the process of life reincarnation being a Divine reality, which reside in the mind of the believer and not in the Divine Mind that know of the meaning and purpose of life and death.

There is nothing Divinely Spiritual about the belief in reincarnation, what is divinely spiritual about life, is that it is the continued birthing of life and not the recycling of life.

Spirituality reflect the action of the body life attitude and behavior while in the act of living and is able to reflect the lives of those that are attached to the sequence of your body life present action of living.

So the purpose of life is not to live life with expectation of returning after death, but is to live it in the presence of death, and live it to experience the Greater Good you can offer to your life, not tomorrow or the wait for your return after death, but for the today that you are certain of.

Divine Sexuality

Chapter 10

Sexuality is more than an act of physical intimacy even though intimacy is the greater and higher expression of your spirituality.

Many of us have taken spirituality and sexuality to be two different acts of expression when in the pursuit of life Greater Good in life, but the two is mutually inclusive to each act of the body life, applying equally to the male (staff gender) as well as the female, (womb gender) the two constituting the One gender in life interaction.

So, when it come to the feminine gender, what does it mean for her to be Divinely sexual expressive, well it mean a whole host of things in term of her personality and the way she Thinks about her self and about her life action that is revealed by her spirituality meaning the way that she act and behave in life.

A woman of Divine sexual qualities is in love with her self first, she first give love (Divine thought) to her self and she make sure that she appear in the most feminine way when expressing her spirituality and her sexuality.

The Divine Spiritual woman is pristine and highly hygienic, she is particular about every aspect of her self appearance, and when she walks, it is with the grace of ease.

Her facial expression is as radiant as the sun, and her smile can say more than a million words can say to you.

Her eyes are as a laser beam penetrating the object she focus upon and her body movement is as the earth revolving around the sun with the greatest of ease and grace and all of her action serve to become apparent, because of her Divine Spirituality that she convey and express by her body action.

The divine spirituality expressed by a Divine woman is presented to be the most sexual display of a woman, when she walks into a room.

The divine woman is seen and do not need to be heard, so when the two acts are of Divine quality, there is a magnetic field that she cause to roam the room by her presence, it all being stimulated by her Divine Spirituality which is a revealing expression her sexuality.

The feminine gender is of a magnetized quality but she can reduce her self to her lowest realm of her magnetic force, meaning when that happen, her Divine Spirituality can not be detected and such a woman that has lost her Divine spirituality become just a woman barren of her Divine sexuality, and that is the life of a Divine feminine gender who no longer have the glow of her divinity.

A woman lost of her divine spirituality has no sexual appeal she has lost the grace of her life and her life become just a show without a Divine appeal and her presence no longer magnetize you, it all just become driven by the sense of your awareness of her, because her Divine Spirituality does not precede her in her coming appearance, meaning that she carry the sign that she is no longer in love with her self.

A woman sexuality is a delicate walk and all women are not qualified to walk that divine spiritual walk, it require full confidence in her ability to reason rationally and logically and she rebuke nor does she disrespect her feminism.

she cuddle it and embrace it, allowing not her vain feminine ego to play a part in her life, that ability of mind self control can only happen when she is being Divinely Spiritual.

Which mean that she is in full charge of her mind and have no desire to be no more than what she has been produced to be, which is the Sun to the masculine gender, he being the earth of man that is meant to revolve around the sun shine of his life, the feminine gender, goddess of the universe.

Just as the planets seem to make haste toward the sun as if they have a meaning and purpose of need to feel secure and protected by the Sun, sometime referring to it as being the Dog Star, the mother of all of her planets, as she is protective of all of her children that hurry toward her for consolation as they submit to the beckon call of the Goddess of the Universe, the Sun Star.

The Sun Star being the Feminine Divine entity of the universe, wrapped in all of her sexuality, as her Divine radiant Spirit reverberate throughout her solar system, which she is in charge of and is making love to her self so that she may remain spiritual and sexually charged to emit the energy needed to summon and protect her children and keep them on their given path to travel to her.

So is it meant for that relationship to be between the feminine and masculine gender when it is all done in an environmental atmosphere of Divine Spirituality, a display of an exuberant attitude and behavioral expression toward each other?

Divine sexual spirituality should be charged and intimate activated by the mind through which all is displayed by your body life action and is done so by the mind direction.

So you see, you need to be careful about who you share your mind energy with or allow to take control of your mind, because it is the quality of your mind that serve as evidence that such a mind action is about the expressing of your Divine Spirituality and such an expression is not of the same quality of mind that is capable of expressing a profane spirit.

The mind you are in possession of must be that of a Divine quality because a Divine mind is not in need of controlling the Divine spirit it reveal, and a profane mind generate thoughts that are not present in the process of Divine thinking, and if it is, then it mean that you no longer have control of your Divine Sexual Spirituality, because you need to be in control of your Divine Mind in order to be in control of your Divine sexuality.

The most Divine spiritual act is sexual intimacy, it is the most profound verification that the energy of the sun goddess has summon the masculine planet it dressed in all of his Divine Spiritual Sexuality.

He is constantly summoned to revolve around the Sun Star in her spatial universe in her mental solar system where she resides and is of her spatial heaven.

The universe by its action is what cause the action for Divine production, it bringing forth the birthing of a new sun (Daughter) and a new planet (Son) and such a union symbolizing that which has been made to be two, is now one again, as is the verification of all things that intimately connect and have the ability to produce while being in such a related position with each other of a different function.

The two have a relationship to the One Divine Essence whose Divine Intelligent Energy is the generator that cause all things to be in motion and to intimately connect and give birth to that which come from such an interaction, an action that can be seen and not seen while in the expression of its sexuality.

It is the Divine sexuality of the infinite universe that produce the goddess of the physical universe, she representing her sexuality to be the Sun-Star and is the goddess that give birth to the planets that become a part of the physical universe, occupying a portion of space which is the body of the Infinite universe of Darkness, it being the existence of the Divine Essence. (GOD)

All things done in the physical universe should be done to reflect your Divine Sexual Spirituality, be you of the feminine or the masculine gender.

SEXUAL TANTRA (tantalize) / FOREPLAY:

When engaged in sexual play such a game should not be played with no intention of actual consummation in your action, unless there is a consent of understanding by those engaged in the game.

Because, unless there is mutual agreement to what extent the game will be played with no desire to consummate, such sexual play can become very dangerous and is without Divine intent.

Tanta / sexual foreplay can be liken to playing with nitro glycerin, the slightest error can cause great devastation to the players if the intent is not honorable and Divine.

Such a game involve being an exhibition in being sexual explicit, sometime visual and sometime touching affection, which can cause sexual arousal and desire.

So by engaging in such a sexual game without the goal being sexual interlocking, I strongly advise to refrain from engaging in such a sexual game as that, because there is nothing Divinely Sexual about Tanta foreplay activity, if the goal is not a reward of Divine Sexual intimacy or to gain some form of sexual grad faction.

DIVINE MASCULINE SEXUALITY:

The masculine gender sexuality should be of such to compliment and not to control the feminine sexuality, the way the universe is arranged, such a dominance of character is not of the Divine spirit of the universe.

It is the Sun Stars that rule and serve as the goddess of the universe and there is nothing that is weak about the Stars, yet they are meek in their powerful action, never failing to rise every morning and set every evening and the planets always making their way to the mother goddess Star.

Regarding the masculine sexuality, there is nothing brute about it, when engaging the feminine gender, he also must be cognizant of himself and how he conduct himself in the presence of himself first.

Because any man who does not have self respect is a man incapable of respecting the feminine gender and respect of the woman come from the man who is at peace with his sexuality.

So to be at peace with your sexuality require you to be in complete confidence in expressing and displaying your Divine spirituality, which rebuke the display of vain ego, envy, jealousy, all done with malice.

The sexuality of the masculine gender is meant to compliment with grace the sexuality of the feminine gender in term of Divine sexual Spirituality, and such does not take away from either gender Divine spiritual sexuality.

Each gender opposite act to compliment the other and not to control and dominate the other, because to do so takes away from your Divine Spirituality and it is your Divine Spirituality that cause your Sexuality to be Divine and attractive.

The masculine gender when being Divinely spiritual serve to be protective of the feminine gender from all who come in attempt to take advantage in a disrespectful way, of the Divine spiritual sexuality of the goddess of the universe, always in haste is the masculine gender to encircle the Divine spirituality of the feminine gender, with his presence.

It is as if to say to all who would come with malevolence, to be aware of the honor and obedience the Divine masculine gender has for the feminine Divine spiritual sexuality.

This is not to imply that the feminine gender is not capable of occupying her space with confidence, by her own action, she being the supplier of the energy that goes out to summon the masculine gender, assuring his coming with a sexuality that is Divinely Spiritual and consuming all who come to her other wise with evil intent.

When the masculine gender is engaging intimately with the feminine gender and that engagement is Divinely spiritual the ease of the opening of the heaven is with such grace and ease that cause only the result of such a union to be the evidence of the Divine significance of the astounding beauty that such a romantic union will bring forth.

As if to serve as evidence of the miracle that such a union can produce, while creating a euphoria from such a Divine Spiritual union that can not be compared by any other unifying connection between two Beings who are of the opposite gender, they being made to become One, in expressing such a Divine Spiritual Sexual union.

ABSTINENCE:

A FALSE PREMISE HAS BEEN ESTABLISHED ABOUT SEXUAL INTIMACY AND IT IS CALL SEXUAL ABSTINENCE FOR RELIGIOUS AND / OR SELF PUNISHMENT REASON.

In religion, it is taught to be a high spiritual virtue to enter into war with nature and in such a war it will cause you to become more favorable to God.

Nothing can be further from the truth than that, as a matter of fact sexual abstinence is not a spiritual act but is a profane act to challenge the natural urges that are produced by intuitive urges that generate a desire to become sexual intimate.

There is no greater energy that makes you to be aware of things involving your body life than your intuitive energy, nature library of the soul.

When there is a physical threat to your life that prevent engagement in sexual intimacy then there is no dispute about what decision you are to make regarding that involvement, because the decision is in favor of life and its pleasure, more so than life desire for pleasure.

There is no greater act in regard to life than to protect your life at all cost, because that is required for you to do so.

But to engage in the highest expression of your Divine Spirituality in an act of self induced abstinence, for no more than to punish your self by denying your self of the basic fundamentals of life activism, is to swear allegiance to a belief system that teach you to ignore Nature callings in life.

Such an act become an evil act unto your self and does not gain you points with the Divine essence, with your religious God maybe, but not the Divine Essence.

Divine Spirituality is not of that which rebuke nature but strive to know and understand nature and all of its body life attributes, and when it come to Divine Spiritual Sexuality, nothing is more Holy and Sacred than your Divine Spirituality.

Because it put you in motion to express your self in Divine Harmony, Order, and Balance, and when in your Body life, you are living, it should be a Divine Spiritual life and such a life does not rebuke nature but adhere to nature with Divine obedience.

Now it is the feminine gender responsibility to induce and require such a Divine Spiritual undertaking as being divinely sexual, because there are many masculine genders as well as feminine genders who are inclined to try and take advantage of your Divine sexuality.

So when you see that to be the case, then you knows that person is not in Divine Spiritual Harmony with you and when that is the case, the act is a selfish and evil one of engagement.

There is no more of an important sexual engagement to enter into than with a Divine Mind, because all that take place in life and is about your life quality, take place in your mind first, even under the influence of your body life senses, it is the mind that end up being your sense destination for completion of the sensation your body life is in pursuit of.

So, that is what makes it so important for you to act by the guidance of your Mind Divine Spirituality and as I have indicated to you, it is no more than the attitude and behavior you express in your body life activity that reveal your spirit.

It is your Divine Sexual Spiritual exoteric display that reveal the quality of your body life way of living, it is the spirituality of your body life self, that is most important to you, because it is what put you on a path of self discovery in a most intimate way.

The mind is what give you the ability to come to know thyself and to be honest when self examining your self, be it of a Divine compliance to nature purity or a evil noncompliance to nature, either way, honesty should be your life goal.

You create your own life impurities when the world is able to look at and make a judgment about you, during the course of your body life living, but it is not the world opinion of you that should motivate you to enter the mental realm that enable you to become Divinely spiritual.

It should be your opinion concerning your body life self, that should hold the greater weight about how you are to be Looked at by the world, as well as how you are to see your body life self.

The spirit you display is what you will see of your self first and it should be to your Divine approval in the way that you think of your self and the decisions that you make for your body life, become you in the making.

Your body life activity through your mind action should be about mastering the spirit that you do convey before the world and that spirit is what enhance your sexual appearance, awareness, and spiritual sexual interaction, be it of the physical or ethereal activity of your body and ethereal life, it being each level of your life activity that display the quality of your Spirituality, be it Divine or profane in spirit.

Change:

Chapter 11

Everybody desire change but not many seem to know in what direction you should go in order to be able to experience the quality of change that will serve to the natural advantage and the Greater Good for your life.

A life that is guided by a Mind that cause you to be divinely spiritual in your life expressed action, is a life that is in order to be able to experience Divine change

CHANGE, THE PROBLEM WITH MANY PEOPLE IS THAT WE DO NOT KNOW WHAT TYPE CHANGE IS BEST FOR LIFE AND WHAT IT MEAN TO LIFE.

THERE ARE TWO TYPE OF EXPERIENCES That CHANGE CAUSE IN LIFE, one that is caused by nature and one that is caused by man, and the change that is caused by man serve to the detriment to those that man has come to control.

So, do I need to point out who it is that man has come to be able to change and control IN THE WORLD, and has caused many in the world to believe as man has taught the world to believe.

There is a certain class of people that mankind control and has influenced them to believe about God, Universe, Self, and did so in a lying and deceiving way.

It is man that has determine what our so call worth in the presence of God is to be and that worth is based upon a man created belief system, which we now have, concerning our selves relationship to the religious God.

A God that we now have been influenced to believe in and about, and it is required that you are to have faith and hope in God, as it has been prescribed by human kind.

Such is the exoteric change from the esoteric knowledge we once knew about, concerning our relationship to the Divine Essence that has no requirement for us to meet and to hold no doubt about the principles of the Divine Truth and Reality.

Those principles were of the knowledge of the Divine Beings during the course of Time when a Divine way of living was lived, which we now today know nothing about, all because of the change we have been made to experience in our way of Thinking about God, the Universe, and our selves, and concerning the Divine relationship the three had with each other when life once was lived Divinely, until man Humanity came and instigated a change in man relationship to the Divine Essence, the two Universe, and Self.

All change is not caused to benefit all that live under a contrived change because many changes we are exposed to effect our ability to Think Divinely, and that is what cause us what to believe about those things we are not thinking about, but is having faith in that we have been changed to believe about, concerning The Divine Essence in life.

If you do not know of your origin and the life we lived before our life came under the change caused by certain types of men with a vile spirit, as they serve to be the master oppressors of our life way of living and believing, then that is proof that we the people do not understand the science of Time, and the change that take place in the natural progressive effective way that it effect our lives.

Tell me, does the Sun change in the order it is designed to live, does the planet change its path that take them in their same cyclical destination and in being a part of the physical universe?

Does the Divine Essence that render to you the Soul energy, change, and is it being that which has caused all things to be in motion?

Do all things alive change from meeting its transformation from life to existence, one is finite and the other is infinite?

All change is not Good change and Good change is what comes to cause you to become the same Divine Being as you once started out to be in life.

Does the saying hold value that say, there is nothing that is new under the sun, is that not an implication of how your life effort should be?

So, if your life have been changed by evil men, then for you to make an effort to return your life back to being the same in its divine spirit that it was when living before the evil of man came and caused your past life way of thinking to become a way of how you now believe about the way your life is to be lived, then such is a change in your life living that is not good change.

Haven't we the people lives been changed for the worse when we allow evil men determine our lives changes that has caused your lives not to be the same as it started out to be on this planet?

Shouldn't you desire your life to be as it first once was, a life that was lived Divinely before it came to be changed by people with evil intent?

All change is not good change and such a change to your life way of living caused by evil men, is not good change.

Change in the natural course of life does not affect your original way of living. it only cause that way of living to maintain its life action until the natural course of change take place in your life.

That is the change that takes you from living naturally to the close of that change, which takes you from your physical way of living to your non physical state, the state of eternal existing, a state of action that is not of the corporeal physical way of living.

So we the people, you who do not desire to convert back to the way nature has allowed you to live in Time Past, a way of living that was Divinely Spiritually and you did Think naturally in the action of your original way of living.

It is your present way of living that has come to cause you not to know thyself, you who are no longer aware of how effective Time is to our life changes and that is what has caused us to be in many ways, in need for the natural change to take place again in our lives, a change that will be divine and not profane to our lives way of living today.

A mind that is fixed to the change caused by certain type of men that have come to be the oppressors of the lower class life, then change in a society has forced you to become servant unto man.

Such is an evil mind that assures the made to be less fortunate to be the prisoner of man made change, and only through natural change will we all encounter the change that nature action bring to your body life.

Changes and you, will cause you to see yourselves changing from a profane life way of living to a Divine way of living, and eventually into the divine state of existence, it being the inert ethereal state of not Being, and it is that state that will put you into the Divine ethereal dimension of an eternal existing state of esoteric infinity, where change is not happening.

It is the changes that life goes through naturally that is Divine, all other changes will be surreal, a quality of change that is not a Divine change and that profane change is caused by evil men action.

It is man made changes which give cause to effect and disfigure our lives, yet the change we seek today in our lives are not a change that will be of Divine quality any more, but of a religious quality, and it is that religious change that has caused us not to be able to know the difference today, between religion and Divine Spirituality.

That is why the world is going through the changes it is experiencing today, a world now full of evil and with a belief system that is not following the natural course that the world is to take, that is if the world is seeking its Divine Spiritual ability to change.

It is the evil world of today that now affects our lives in a horrible and profane way today, which is preventing the world from experiencing its Divine Spirituality.

Without a change back to our Divine way of living we will continue to experience a spirit that is the cause for all of the crisis that occur in our lives today, caused by the profane relationship the world now express toward each other and have caused the world from displaying a Divine Spirituality today.

It has already been stated in this book that all change is not desirable change and desirable change come to those who humbly seek the mental path that lead to the ability to express a Divine Spirit that indicate the way we live our lives.

Which is a living that we will put on display, a life that is expressed divinely spiritual and whose only natural change will be to enter the final stage of the Body Life Divine final action, which is transitioning into the Divine Ethereal eternal state of existing infinity, a change that we all will encounter in our life Time.

So it is Divine to seek and experience change that is natural to your life way of living and it will be such a life living experience that will determine the quality of life you will live, and by such a display, your life will reveal the quality of your Spirituality and that quality of living will indicate and represent the quality of Mind that guide your Body Life.

So the question is, will it be a Mind capable of profane spiritual expression or will it be a Mind that is capable of revealing your body life Divine Spirituality?

You have the responsibility to choose the quality of mind that you will allow to guide your life in a world seemed to have gone mad, and perform evil deeds toward each other in the world today.

Conclusion

Chapter 12

In this final act to put all of this I have shared with you in this book into a concise precise perspective so that some semblance of order will give you the ability to know and understand what has been shared with you about that motion we refer to as life.

Life being a motion formed and shaped in a very unique fashion with a body mass that is given the ability to reason, using a process that the entity in motion, in the form of matter, is given the ability to think and to form your thoughts in such a way it give you the ability to reason rationally and to be logical when in search for the Divine Truth, and to know what is Divinely Real.

Such an ability coming from the stimulation of what is accepted to be the sense mind coordination, is what put all of those things that confront our lives in some kind of orderly perspective, but do not succeed all of the Time in such a pursuit to know of and to understand the motion call life.

So when the question comes in an inquisitive way asking what is Life meaning and purpose, and what is that life in motion objective, and is it left up to you who live your life, to determine the answers to life meaning?

The answer is an undoubtedly yes.

This book has attempted to answer those questions, now whether it has been done successful or not, that is left up to you the reader to decide.

This book has attempted to convey to you that life, after all is said and done about it, happen to be a simple pursuit, which is just as it has been given to you.

So it is your responsibility to live your life so that it will serve to be a Divine pleasure to you and any life that is not lived freely, is a life that has been interfered with by a force other than the force that has given life to you.

So when you allow evil forces to enter into your life, it mean that your ability to reason rationally and logically has been interrupted by a life that is of the same form and fashion that you are, the phenotype may be different but the life ingredients are the same as your life.

Such a life force is no different than you are in term of its form and it has been constructed by the laws and forces of Nature and yet it is that Divine action of events given to be a part of our lives by the Divine Essence that has caused all life to be, but play no part in the decision we make in our lives.

The one driving force of the body life is its Mind, an energy of a distinct action in performance, it is in the body and is the cause of the organs of the body life to function.

That same energy is what is flowing throughout the Body giving to it life and in the brain organ it is the energy of life that have the brain sending signals that cause the various body parts to function and cause you to have a mind.

It is the Mind that gives meaning to life even though the life form may be different in its phenotype; its movement is guided by that same energy source that is of the intelligence in the universe.

So, it is given to be accepted that the Mind that express its action of intelligence in the body life in a Divine way, it is a part of the body life and it give you an ability to live your life in Harmony, Order, and Balance, a sign of a body life mind that is functioning reasonable, rationally, and logically, which you must choose to do.

The quality of your mental action is what enhance and demonstrate your Divine Spirituality, which should be your life goal and objective.

Living Divine will open up the many avenues of a mind process and if in a Divine progressive way your mind will and can take you on a inner stellar journey throughout the inner verse (internal equivalent to the Universe) of your internal ethereal existing self, a self that is a entity of the esoteric alchemic dimension of your ethereal mind.

All things of the natural elements flow within your body life, so life objective should be to master the ability to control the thoughts that are formulated by your sense mind coordination, when in use by the body life.

Whether your life use is externally or internally the operative engagement is to control the life processes with your mind, from which is emanating your thoughts and it is the thoughts that send forth the energy that is capable of changing things that are important in order to have your life to be lived in the way it was given, which was Divinely free.

So, not until we learn all over again to think of things not in physical term but in ethereal term and such is being in nonphysical term, the level of dimension that put us in connection with what we call the Divine ethereal world.

The divine ethereal world is the internal self where such a world being not of this outer physical world but is the world of alchemy, esoteric, and intuitive energy action, and all of such action being in a state of eternal existence.

Such an action being in the dimension of eternal infinity consisting of the same energy that give motion to your body life as well as to your ethereal inert existence, one is physical and the other is nonphysical, but both is of the Divine intelligence and it is Divine energy that is intelligence.

It is that intelligence that is the cause of an external as well as an internal Divinity and that Divine energy is being of such a Divine spirit until it is not in need of commanding nor is it in a demanding mood to influence your every decision you make about your life.

Such a responsibility is exclusively for your mind to make concerning the action that your body life mind is to decide about how to deal with those things that your life will be confronted with during your life Exoteric Time, while your life is enclosed in the physical garment of your body.

Today, there are so many isms that effect our lives, so much so until we have abandoned our responsibility we are given to have for our lives.

You see, you lose the edge you must have over your life when you assign other people to think and reason for you, meaning that the Mind that came with your body life, it is the mind that now govern your life by the way that you use your mind.

When your spirit is no longer being expressed divinely you now have a mind that govern your life based upon a set of rules that are based upon do this and don't do that, what is right and what is wrong, and those are condescending terms describing and determining what is to be acceptable to your life way of living and what is not to be acceptable in the way that you are to live your life.

Terms that define and restrict your life behavior are not from the Mind that produce a Divine Spirit a spirit that is not in need of life regimented restrictions as has been so developed by an oligarchy of men whose mind determine the way and how they believe during the course of your life.

The world has been structured, and it is in such a way that it express the spirit the world has come to be today, under the control of the few that now rule the world.

It is the few among us that now tell us how we the people of the world is to conduct themselves in life, in a way that meet the specification of the few that control the thought processes of the world society today.

In a world society where the people have been given the impression that it is the people that make the decisions that govern their lives and the people have been given a litany of beliefs to support that impression.

Those beliefs are set forth by an institution call religion, it to being the creation of the minds of the few that has come to be above the world society and remaining inconspicuous to the people that make up the world, while the few in the world influence the decisions you are making about the way you should live your life.

That mean whomever control your mind, control your life, and under such condition, the spirit you display is the spirit that is not born from you having control of your mind.

It is the spirit of those few that are in control of your mind and as it has been shared in this book, it is the mind that governs your life decisions that you make in life.

Your life submission to someone other than your self begin with the way you are conditioned to believe and not know about the Divine Essence and how the Universe was formed and about the oligarch of men who know that if they can get you to believe in the theory they have about God and the Universe, then your life no longer is your life.

Your life would have become the life that is under the control of the few and the powerful that govern the world, so let us call this the beginning of the world under the domination of the few and powerful in the world.

WORLD DOMINATION:

The world is dominated by an oligarchy of men and they set their lies about God and the Universe based upon the creation of their God and their rendition to the world about how the Universe begin.

Stating to the world that God is a God based upon Right and Wrong and that the Universe started with a Big Bang, as if the universe became the alchemy action from such a bang, indicating that the universe came into being by the performance of magic performed by God, a God that is created by the oligarchy of men for purpose to become rulers of the world.

First of all the Divine Essence (GOD) is not to be dictated to nor is the Divine Essence to be second guessed about its Reality, Meaning, and its Purpose to all it has caused To Be.

The Divine Essence need no religious foundation to establish a belief system about its existence, and as for as the nonphysical infinite Divine Universe is concerned and its Divine existence, it has always been as it appear to you today.

The Divine infinite universe is a Mass Of Energy Consisting Of The Infinite Space Darkness and as for the physical universe is concern it is of a continuous coming forth out from and going back into the Infinite Universe.

It is the solar systems consisting of Stars and have Planets revolving around those stars that make up of the physical universe that come forth from the nonphysical infinite universe that is a process of continuous addition and subtraction of all of its parts.

So based upon the theory about God and the Universe and who and what they are, which is no more than a theory about God and the universe action.

The origin about the universe came from an oligarchy of men, which is how those few men of great wealth and power came to be in domination and control over the world.

When a few people are able to control the world thoughts about what to believe about God and the Universe and by the world having been beaten into submission to adopt such a religious belief, and when such a control over the mind of the world is under control of the few in the world.

Your thoughts then are no longer your thoughts and your Spirituality is no longer divine but has been converted to become mentally religious and it is religion that set out to dominate the Mind thoughts of the World today.

When dealing with the Divine Essence you have no need to describe, define, or prove ITS Existence, such is the power of assurance that the Divine Essence has, because the fact that you can wonder and get to know about the Divine Essence, such is the proof that the Divine Essence Is Real and True.

It is the Divine Essence that does not influence you in the way it has caused you to be and that is with free will and choice, and it is the choice you make that you should be most concerned about in your body life.

Because, it is your life that can be dominated and influenced to choose and believe as the oligarchy of men in power will have you to believe about God and the Universe, both of the universe, the nonphysical and the physical.

You should never allow your mind to become dominated by other than your self because to do so you lose control over your life and if you are not in control of your life, that mean you have lost control of your mind and by not being in control of your mind you set your self up to believe anything someone else tell you about your self.

So it is the spirit your body life display under those circumstances that is not of Divine spirit, a display of the quality of your mind from which will be revealed, coming from a none influenced mind and it being the mind that your body life must always remain to have under your body life control, that is, if you desire to experience your Divine Spirituality.

KNOW THYSELF:

Getting to know thyself is not an easy task, especially if you have allowed your mind to become under somebody else domination that is other than your self.

Here again, it is about the Mind and I will continue to remind you that without control of your mind, your life become a life of misery full of uncertainties.

So without control of your mind you can not experience your Divine Spirituality and when your spirit is not of Divine action, then your mind is under the control of profane action and in such a state of mind there is in no way you can get to know thyself.

It is knowledge that open the mental gateway into the inertly ethereal dimension of your inner verse (inner action of the mind self) travel, a journey that will reveal and enable you to see the things that are pertaining to the Divine Essence, to the Universe, and the entire cycle of your life activity that happen in the past and is happening in the present.

The past and present is to be such of a mind action that will be able to cause you to become aware of thyself, a knowledge that is necessary, if you are to understand the alchemic and esoteric avenues of happening in your Divine Mind.

Your Divine mind being a mind that is required of you, that is if you are to experience your Divine Spirituality.

Early on in this book I have shared with you what the spirit truly is and how it is a representation of your mind thoughts and not some ghostly ethereal entity that move around in and out of your body in an ethereal image of your self, as been so depicted by many who speak about spirit.

There are people who lead you to believe that the spirit is the ethereal body of your physical body self and because such a description of the spirit has been planted in your conscious mind and the mind being the energy that it is, and the power it possess.

The energy can cause the mind to have the ability to create such an image of the spirit and can place it in locomotion to become as the mind conscious has been programmed to believe the spirit to be.

We have been told that the spirit is an image of our self, as we go through life believing in a way about the spirit as it has been projected to you to be and you question not.

Since this is a book about Divine spirituality and by specifying Divine Spirituality, such imply about the expression about the Spirit, and the spirit when being expressed, it is not automatically Divine but can be of a profane expression as well as a divine expression.

The spirit is a display of your mind action that is reflecting your thoughts by the body of your life action, it is what reveal an image of you that is of a Divine display of expression of your mind thoughts or the spirit can be a profane display of your body life expressed action.

The spirit is being expressed by your mind and it is your mind that is projecting an image of you that is being displayed by your expressed attitudinal behavior that is coming from the mind thoughts process.

Such a process is what reveals the spirit image coming from the action of your body life and is displayed so all can be looked at.

Just as there is a Divine Spirit which reveal the quality of your spirituality, so it is that there is an evil spirit that reveal there being an evil spirituality, each is revealed by you, by the way that you express your self and your expression is the revelation of your self which reveal the quality of the thoughts that are emanating out from your mind action.

So that is why it is important that you strive to become in control of your mind because it is your mind that is responsible for the quality of life you will live while in the form of your physical body, which is alive because of the energy that flow through the body.

Divine Spirituality is a phenomena that emanate from an energy action process that is capable of developing its action into a sense and thinking process.

Such a process is no more than the energy revealing its action in different methods of processes, those methods of process becoming what is referred to as the mind that is of the energy action by body displayed expression,.

Such an energy expression is to be made manifest by the body life that is done so by a displayed expressed manner of the body life action.

It is all being the body displayed expression that is being done by the way the body portrays itself by its life action.

So it is important in the way that you train your mind self to think about all that your body sense mind reveal to you and all that the mind is capable of reminding and projecting to you that is beyond the body life inter play between the sense mind interaction.

The Mind reveal to you the spirit of your body life living in an exoteric manner of mental expression, displaying the way the body life is acting and behaving in and toward many and various situations that are being experienced by your body life, expressed by the mind and spirit body action.

So in order to master the knowledge of thyself you must know of the inner working of your energy action which is capable of revealing to you the true, real, and Divine Nature of thyself, both physical as well as spiritual.

The quality of such a spirit that is being displayed in such a way will be the cause for your mind to be conducted Divinely and to be able to function Divinely thoughtfully.

The mind is that which must be under your control and not under somebody else control, such is required in order for you to experience your Divine Spirituality and that is what become evidence that you now know thyself.

FREEING THE MIND:

There is nothing in life that affect your life that can escape from passing through the mind process, the processing may not always be accurate but the mind is in awareness of it and sometime you may not remember certain things that happen to you but it does not mean that it did not pass through the processes of your mind.

So it is highly important that your body life move freely in relationship with your mind which is energized by the energy that moves freely throughout the body and is effecting each vital part of your body organs.

The Divine Energy is what gives the body the appearance of life with the ability to reason and to make decisions in life, be they rational or irrational decisions such a mind in use is what measure the level of the body life expressed intelligence.

A free mind produce a free spirit but it does not have anything to do with the quality of that spirit, such depend upon how well you are in the know of thyself which depend on how much in control of your mind that you are experiencing.

As you come into this world you come with a mind that is not burden with precondition even though the mind is not blank as many people have been led to believe it is, because in the early stage of life growth and development, the sense to mind relationship is that of innocence, but it is not to say that the energy that flow through an infant mind hold back its information from the infant.

Therefore implying that the infant is not in possession of a mind because of its physical stage of growth and development is not natural to me because as for as I am concerned there is no mind that is ever blank.

You might not be able to process what is moving over the mind wave which prevent you from being ready to interpret the information that is flowing to constitute the mind action, yet the infant by being expressive indicate a mind presence while not yet ready to verbalize what the sense to mind is revealing at an early stage of growth and development which does not verify that the mind is not in action.

It is the early stage of life which makes the mind to be free from being influenced in making decisions about what the sense to mind is revealing when the mind is of such a young developing and innocent state of your body life growth and development.

It is all because there has not been Time enough for the developing body life to become opinionated about what the sense to mind is revealing at such an early stage of the body life development.

So based upon the dynamic relationship that is going on between the body life sense to mind interaction, the mind in the child early stage of its body life is a mind that is free of all life regiments that interrupt that mental cycle of freedom from decision making that is based upon a created set of rules that are formed by man made predetermine set of values that dictate a set described discipline for your body life, all of which you must adhere to in life.

It is dictated to you the way you must behave in certain life situations and such restrictions are what form a mind that is not free to be creative in guiding your own life and causing it not to be independent from the way others have guided your life in the way it must go, which does in fact effect the quality of spirit that will be associated with your body life expression.

A free mind is a mind that has received salvation coming from the soul and it being a mind that is a part of the soul energy, an energy that is Divine in its action and it is such a mind that set its own values and conceive of its own course for your body life to take.

All such mental action must be in compliance to the Divine action that is in display by the universe Divine action, it being of stars and planets, elements seen and not seen.

The universe is to be the master teacher, instructing us in the way we should behave in life, it serving as an example how we are to relate one to the other and to know the

Divinity in our different form and the nature of our Being, which is designed to remain one to each other.

Only a Free Mind is capable of taking us into the various quadrants of our mind, giving such a Divine mind the ability to perform many and different action of revelation about the going on in our past and present life experiences, which give the mind ability to be capable of taking you into the infinite dimension where the Spirit of the Divine Essence reside and is in continuous ethereal inert existence, intrinsic within the alchemy of the Eternal Darkness.

So in order to be able to change conditions in the world and thus our lives, it require that freedom of the mind is a must, in order to effect constructive Divine change and change in our mind way of performing is required, that is if the world is to survive.

We must live a Divine way of life, as it was originally designed to be performed by the Divine Essence of all things.

Freedom of mind must be allowed to function in such a way that it allow the mind to wander as well as wonder, wander into the dimensional abyss of the unconscious past and the conscious present.

The mind must be able to express and display an attitude that wander throughout the inner verse of your body life, as well as throughout the external universe that have been set in the spatial heaven.

It is the mind that is expressing a behavior that cause it to wonder about all the mind in its travel is revealing mentally and is doing so in such a way it cause the mind to see those things that are happening and have happen over the course of your life.

It is the attitude and behavior coming from the mind action and it is the mind that must be in a Divine mood, and that mood is what reflects the Divine spirituality of your mind performance.

It is that Divine Mind that is able to wander into such ethereal and inert dimensions and wonder about all that the mind is capable of seeing all of that which is of those various levels of dimensions, that is what cause you to be able to experience and see such a phenomena taking place in your mind eye.

Such an happening require for your mind to be free in its action that is revealed and guided by the Divine spirit.

It is the mind action that is taking place on the exoteric as well as on the esoteric level of your free mind action, taking place in a Divine performance that is happening because of the freedom of your mind thoughts, that which cause you to be able to perform in such a Divine Spiritual way.

DIVINE ENERGY:

All that we do in life and all that life really consist of is Divine Energy, Divine because the energy performance is operating in Harmony, Order, and Balance, and it cause all Spatial bodies and ethereal elements by their action to be Divine.

Those bodies performance is depended upon the spirit that they display by their body movement, and the movement of their bodies are caused by the Divine energy within, but the bodies spirit is not dictated by the energy that cause the attraction of the bodies to each other.

All of those moving bodies are being summoned by the stars of the universe, based upon the difference between the stars and planets, and yet they all have a common relationship to each other.

Those Spatial bodies performance is based on how well they are submitting to the more powerful attracting bodies in the universe, they being the stars that have charted a course path to be adhered to in a Divine action of movement for the planets.

Those attracting bodies being the opposite to those bodies that they are attracting, and all such bodies that make up the physical universe is there because of that One Divine Essence Energy, and it does not dictate.

The Divine Energy just generate the energy needed for all universal bodies to perform, but the quality of those bodies performance is depended on how well those bodies relate to each other and all Beings are a part of the physical universe and all of its members are being effected by each other action .

All things in form and out of form is of the Divine Essence Making, and we all are the sum total of the Divine Essence, all having intelligence even though it may not be of the same quality expressed in the same way by all forms of life but it does not change the fact that it is the Divine Energy that is intelligence.

There is no different classification of Divine Energy and there is Only Divine Energy, and there is no Good Energy or Bad Energy and the level of our intelligence is depended on how we will choose to use our mind energy when making decisions for our Body Life.

FREEDOM OF MIND:

The greatest virtue of all that will bring you freedom of mind is Wisdom and wisdom is in having control of thought and your action, and being confidence in your devotion of purpose, and you have confidence in your master teacher that is teaching you about the necessary journey of life that will lead you to experience your Divine Spirituality.

You must also be able to be free of resentment of those that persecute and deceive you and is speaking all manner of evil about you, such a virtue is call fortitude and it allow you to remain steadfast in control of the freedom of your mind in all that you think about and do in life.

So it is the virtue that your body life that you must be the master of, that is what insinuate your Divine Spirituality which when expressed require a freedom of mind and it is that freedom of mind that also incorporate an ability to know what is acceptable to you and what is not acceptable to you.

Your Divine Spirituality also allow you to know what is real and that which is not real and from such a freedom of mind through wisdom, we derive a knowledge about the value of justice and temperance in living a Divine Spiritual Life.

Wisdom is Life Crown and without it knowledge and understanding is no where to be founded because from such come the arrival of wisdom which serve as evidence that you have mastered the virtuous mental cardinal points that is required of you, in order for you to experience the highest quality level of your mind action which reveal your Divine Spirituality which is expressed by your Body Life Living.

Attitude and Behavior must be of Divine virtue if you are to get to Divinely correspond with Nature, Self, Universe, and the Divine Essence, (GOD) such a relationship with those entities are required if you are to enjoy the greater good of life, which is the purpose of living.

Without the freedom of mind a virtuous life is not possible to live and it is the virtues you are to master in life that will elevate you into the mental realm of Divine Truth and Reality and anything less will put you on the phenomenal path of not Divine Reality but Virtual reality, a reality that give off the effect of being real but in fact is not real and that become the phenomenon of nature illusion of reality.

It is the actual fact of the things that is not seen of the inner nature of things that are real and not that which the conceived idea about the things that are perceived of is taken to be real.

It is the freedom of mind that arrange the order of your life living divinely and it being no more than a thoughtful and intuitive awareness revealing the manner in which you will conduct and live your life with freedom.

A mind being the most important aspect of your life living and it being your life living virtues that will determine the way you will live your life, and it being the quality of your life living that will determine the quality of your Life Spirituality.

All things of nature come from an action that actually bring forth the effect of the material fact that affect your life, and those things are coming from the freedom of your mind thoughts, which is what cause you to conceive of the idea about the immaterial fact that is giving the material affect of things being the fact we call reality.

Freedom of mind is what determines the quality of your life and the way you will live your life will be by the phenomena of principals created by you.

You now use numbers and alphabets, and they being no more than symbols used in such a way that they are arranged to define and measure what is deemed to be the fact of a matter.

So what is to be moral and immoral to measure our freedom by, we end up having a numerical code of conduct to determine what is factual true and real, and that is how and what we govern our life by to determine to what extent our freedom is allowed in living our lives..

Life is meant to always reflect some measure of Divinity that verify a freedom of mind in action, and it is that quality of mind that reveal a spirit of life that is expressing an action of mind that is causing and guiding your life to be in harmony, order, and balance, in a society that is in a divine relationship with each other. `

Remember, it is the soul, mind, spirit, that reveal the character of your body life, and it is your body life that operate on a conscious and subconscious level, which is what reflect the quality of your mind freedom.

But to be able to become aware of your past and present lives action, that is the sum total of your ethereal and physical body self, it is from those two dimensions where such information come from that reveal things about your life and the inner inert ethereal level of your inner ethereal self, which is beyond the level of consciousness.

Such divine existing information is not made known by your mental action but you are made to be aware of such unassisted revealed Divine information by direct revelation from the soul to an intuitive inert ethereal esoteric inner action, constituting your inner ethereal self, it being the inert action that take place in your body life, without you playing a part in its doing!!!

Some people call such awareness, dae'javue, (familiar with the unfamiliar) knowing and remembering without a thoughtful level of the various level of conscious involvement.

Such an inert ethereal action is the level of inner dimension, where Divine Truth and Reality reside, in the existing spatial eternal infinite universal non-dimensional alchemic level.

There is where Truth and Reality is in constant uninterrupted motion, an action at the ultimate infinite height where Divine freedom of Revelation come from, such is the infinite height, depth, width and length where the Divine Essence reside.

So the purpose of your body life is not to bring salvation to the soul, the soul is never in captivity.

So freedom must be of the mind because it is the mind from where the processes of your Divine and profane thoughts emanate from, and that is why you should always be of a Divine wisdom that will cause you to be in control of your thoughts, and they will be divine thoughts incubating and being born from your Divine mind.

Such a divine mental status of your mind require the freedom of mind and it is your mind that you must be in control of at all Time, if not, then there will be an alternating of Divine and Profane evil thoughts that can cause the body life to be a life of living confusion and it is such a life that is not the living of a Divine Spiritual Being.

GODDESS AND GOD:

First allow me to share with you that the term goddess and god that is assigned to you, is based upon the quality of spirit that is displayed by you.

Goddess and god is a term given to the female and male who are in motion to reclaim your Divine Spiritual status, there is nothing alchemic about the status of being a goddess or god.

Therefore, the power that each will posses will not come from some magically possession of a term that classify you, but it will come from you being in possession of virtuous wisdom that reveal that you are in control of your mind.

The divine quality of your mind, that will be the result that will cause you to be a virtuous Being, a goddess or a god of nature, depending on your gender classification.

Therefore, such a status is verified by your Spirit and to become a goddess or a god, you must exemplify such a life style that will verify the quality of your attitudinal behavioral display, and I will attempt to deal with each status separately, first with the status of a goddess.

The goddess is of no greater status than the masculine god, and vice versus, and each is to function in its own sphere of travel, one meant to compliment the other and not to be in possession of the other.

We are only talking about a Title here, which is to identify the level and quality of wisdom that is in your mind possession, but the goddess does have a certain attracting quality about her, but only when she is sending out her Divine magnetic energy field and that energy is generated by her virtuous spirit.

A goddess is the feminine gender with a Divine spirit and her life action is that of being full of divine emotion expression, of Love, devotion, being sentimental, caring, compassionate, and those emotional expressions are what cause you to be able to live a virtuous life of a goddess.

You will become able to see things that the sense can not look at and know of things that only the level of conscious is not involved with, in having you to be aware of events that have happen that your body life is a part of and has been exposed to, and now is a part of your life DNA.

The goddess is able to go into different dimension levels where her body life mental level does not go, she can cause things to happen in, to, and around her life.

It is all because she has full command of her mind which cause her to be virtuous and receptive to her intuitive self.

So to be a goddess is to be Divinely Spiritual, which mean that she is aware of her Divine Essence, it being the Energy Of Divine Intelligence, the soul of your Being, it being the Divine Intelligence of your mental self.

The goddess express the spirit that is of the Divine Essence attributes, which are Harmony, Order, Balance, and that is what cause all things that are produced and is of a physical nature, that cause your body life to be of an intelligent design by Divine intelligence.

So, it is the divine intelligence that is of the Divine Essence and IT IS incorporated inside of all things that are of a physical and nonphysical nature, the former being the illusion of reality and the latter being the Divine Essence, it being the truth and reality of the physical illusion that we experience during our body life living, which is a part of our body life experiences.

For you to make claim to be a goddess, it make such a claim that must be verified by the virtuous spirit that you display in your body life, a claim easily made but a life that is difficult to live, when in an evil and profane environment.

It is the mind that determine the spirit of your environment, so if the environment is to be divine then your mind must be of divine action, because it is your mind action that reveal the quality of your spirit and that it is your mind that must be of Divine quality, in order to wear the title of a goddess or a god.

Masculine God:

The godlike gender is the opposite to the gender of the goddess, but the spirit of the two must be the same coming from each other, and is expressed in the same body life that is of a mental action that is in Harmony, Order, Balance, such is the way that the body life is to live, being full of compassion, sentimental, caring, divinely emotional expression (Love) and all of the mental divine attributes that is to be expressed by the god in his body life living expression.

The god man is he who is in motion around the goddess and he is to be sending out a signal of obedience and acknowledgement to the goddess, with a willingness of submission.

Such a spirit of divine nature is not to be taken as one being weaker than the other, the difference being that one function different than the other, but each is attracted to the other Divinely.

So does this mean that the goddess give energy to the god of her Being, as she is constantly sending forth the energy of magnetism with gravity at the level that it is capable of maintaining a divine action of movement in the universe?

Yes it does, that is the intelligent design of the Universe, done by the Divine Essence, and because of the Divine Essence presence, the physical universe become as it is, it being not the eternal infinite universe but it is the physical universe and all of its parts being connected to each other.

The nature of the god and goddess is to be no different in their Divine expression of their body life living, each of their spirit must be of the same composition as the other.

So the saying that the masculine gender is in possession of the feminine gender and the goddess is in possession of the masculine gender is misleading.

It is as if to say that the star is in the planet and the planet is in the star, disqualifying the two gender differences to each other, by intelligent design, the commonality come to the two gender opposites when the Divine Spirituality is by expressed action and there should be no difference in the goddess Spirituality and the masculine god spirituality, both should be displayed and expressed Divinely, and there is no difference in Divine expression.

In the animate universe the star is the opposite difference to the planet, the star symbolizing the goddess of the universe and the planet the masculine god of the universe with the star goddess being just as attracted to the planet as well as the planet is attracted to the star, so the star send our her arms of energy wave to caress the planets and the planets resist not.

So, by the planets submitting to the call of the goddess star, and each being different from the other, each having their different function in the universe that consist of the stars and planets, which cause such a relationship between the stars and planets to be Divine.

So it is with the god and goddess of the two gender difference that we function and we do so, by the same principle the animate universe function by, and it consisting of visual stars and planets that are in a physical movement that verify Divine function in motion, each object moving in Harmony, Order, and Balance, with and to each other.

Therefore, by the god and goddess being full of their Divinity by their expression it does not change the nature of each of their function and that is what keep them in compliance to the Law of the universe whose principles are based upon the law of difference in function but is the same in the natural composition of the two being physical.

All that are anthropomorphous Beings was at one Time upon this Planet Earth Divine and now should be desirous of becoming Divine again, in the way you live your body life.

Such a desire would put the world back on its original path of cyclical motion and each member acting in compliance to the divine display and expression of the universe, whose law of action is based upon the Divine principles of differences, yet we being in divine relationship with and to each other

THE SOURCE OF LIFE:

Since life seem to be our main concern even to the point that we believe in so many ways of how life came to be and what the source is that give cause for life to be and how it is that we must live our lives in order to be able to escape the action of death, we have come to believe that God give specific instructions of how life is to be lived.

We are told that life must be obedient to God in order to be able to take it into an unknown Dimension, that dimension is where belief has taught you to be a place that life can go and be forever in peace with your life and all others, there is Heaven.

Such has become our motivation for living and it is to be believed that you can save your life from the action of death eternal cessation to life and believe you can transfer your life to a higher plane of dimensional living.

Such a belief is what give you cause for not attempting to live your life divinely here in this physical dimension, where eventually death does come into play with life, in order to bring it to a close and for life to be no more, an action that come escorting the body physical.

Life is for the body and the body in motion is life, and the two have a expiration date that is not transferable.

So let us deal with the source of life many of us have contemplated and now believe about its purpose is to the living and what the reason life serves to the body.

So, the question is, what could be the source of life? Great philosophers have tackled such a notion of wonderment about life, some say that Water is the source of life others say that the limitless and boundless of space is life source.

Well it is my revelation that tells me that Divine Energy is the source of life, as well as to all things looked at and is not seen in the physical.

Life is motion meant to be only for the body in a physical dimensional form, meaning that life is not transferable beyond the physical.

Life in actuality, it is only an illusion any way, and you are capable of causing life to be your reality, so all of the things that your life encounter physically, causing them to appear to be real, is because your mind will it to be real.

There is only one Energy and that Energy is Divine in its action and it is founded and is needed in everything physical and nonphysical, and those things of the energy can and will function differently, but how you function is of no blame to the energy that cause you to be able to function in life.

Energy is the source that give you life and how you express and display your life, it become entirely left up to you, and the decision you make for your life is of no credit or fault to the energy that cause your life to be as your life appear to be by your action.

There are so many lies that have been told about the Divine Energy, some people have been led to believe that there is such an energy that is bad and evil, good and pleasant, energy that lie and deceive, energy that maim and kill, not so.

It is how the energy is used and the way that you use the energy is of no blame of the energy, it just provide to you life, so however you choose to live that life, it is left entirely up to you.

The objective in life should be to achieve the greater good by living your life divinely and not by classifying your life action.

You should use your mind to reach the pinnacle of divine thought and to learn the technique of elevating your mental ability in order to transcend to other dimensions by the use of your thoughts.

You do so, so that you may be able to enter the dimension where there is an absent of thought awareness, which will place you into the abyss of genetic intuitive awareness, it is such an awareness that put you at such a level that is out of mind action.

There is where the Divine Truth and Reality reside, in a dimension that is the limitless and boundless of the space, it being the perfect night. (Dark Energy)

Through and by the source of your life living, which is the divine energy of your life, you are capable of experiencing two dimensions of your Being, they being your physical life and your inert ethereal existence, and there is a difference between the two, one is for the physical aspects of your life living and the other is for the nonphysical aspect of your inner self existence, and one has limits and the other is without limits.

Your physical life is To Be, because of the source of your life, which is the energy that cause you to be alive, and your life is guided by your sense mind activity, that which is given to be what you reveal by the living of your body life.

So in regard to your not physical state of inner self intuitive existence, which come without the assistance of your sense mind action, you are able to be aware of things you played no part in thinking about and such an occurrence take place beyond the life sense mind action, and that become the Divine action of your inner ethereal self

Such an action is called Divine intuitive Interventional informative awareness, a level where you are automatically elevated, and on such a level, there is where you be at the level of your Divine intuitive self, the source of all of your body action being the Divine Energy that dwell inside and around your body life.

It is your inner self inert ethereal existence, and your outer physical self, that is associated with the body life, connected while occupying the same space, that is what gives your body the meaning of life.

It is the two method of action that have the same source, and that same source energy is providing your body with the two method of being aware, an awareness that inform you about your life past and present and that which is beyond life.

It is an awareness that is caused by your sense mind life action and your out of sense mind action, one is caused by the action of the sense mind conscious and subconscious state, and the other is caused by your life inner intuitive self, with the latter dealing with all of your physical and nonphysical dimensions while the former is dealing with the present and past life physical events.

LIFE GREATER GOOD:

In order to obtain life greater good it require that you must obtain the equilibrium between Harmony, Order, and Balance in your life living action.

It is a life living on such a scale that it verify the level of the Greater Good that cause you to know about the frequency of life, it being an action that cause the vibration of your life to resonate with such a divine action at such a level where there is expressed a divine spirit that verify a life of virtuous living.

The divine quality of life is the way of it being an expression of the way it is being lived and it being a life way of living that cause you to experience such a pleasant and joyful life, a life that should be the desire of all intelligent Beings.

You must become set in your Divinity and must not be deterred by deceiving vile vain living in the world, and you should not be easily influenced, because to be so, is a sign that you have yet to be in possession of the mind that is necessary to have the will that will cause you to experience your Divinity.

Becoming Divine is the only life path to travel, it being a path that is a journey you must take in order for you to be able to experience a life way of living enjoying the greater good in life.

A person who do not seek to gain control of the mind is a person who would have justice to escape that person life and a life without temperance is a life full of confusion.

A life absent of wisdom can not become a life that is living divinely and the absent of Divine virtue is a life prevented from experiencing the greater good in your life way of living.

It should be the desire of all intelligent life that is experiencing it divine spirituality to respect your life so much until you will protect your life at what ever cost it will take to do so.

Life is for the body and it should be used to experience the greater good and greater value in life and it is life that does not transfer beyond life realm, which is of the physical.

so suffering is not a natural state of life way of living and to suffer is to punish life and since life is a gift given by the Divine Essence, then life is to be revered and honored at all Time.

Life is not to be just any gift but it is a Divine Gift, worthy to be praised as it revolves in the status of its Spiritual Divinity.

Life was never meant to be anything other than to be Divine and life natural measurement requires Divine calculation.

It is said that the universe is about numbers and I would rather think that numbers are all about the universe, no more than symbols to represent the universe in action and to measure the attitudinal behavioral movement of those moving lively objects that consist of the universe.

It is because of the Divine movement of the universe that the universe express its Greater Good, by the action of its motion and by its relationship each object is to each other and those objects in the universe is what make up the universe.

All of those universal objects are moving about together in the one limitless eternal infinite space which causes the circle (Zero) to be the greatest of all numeral symbols of the symbolic sequence of number numerology.

The mind is the doorway through which you exit in order to enter the domain of the greater good and such a good, dwell within the perfect eternal infinite limitless Night, escaping the tentacles of a mind that constantly war against your natural state of Divinity.

The mind being the mind being the action that identify the symbols as numbers that bind all universal objects together, those objects are parts that constitute the physical universe.

Need I remind you of the fact that there are two universes, one infinite while the other is finite and one is not physical and the other is physical?

There are also two of yourself, one physical and the other not physical and it is the not physical of yourself that is Divinely true and Real and it being that Divine Real self that you be trying to get in touch with in all of your acts of meditation.

When you meditate it should be for the purpose to get beyond the mind and into the dimension of your Divine intuitive self, requiring you to be vitreous in such a divine undertaking, which is what cause you to be able to enter the sanctity of your inner dimensional self.

Yet, just like the Infinite Universe never leave the boundless infinite spatial night, your Divine Real Self never leave you, it is there present inside of you, alternating with the physical action of yourself, the self that is not Real and will eventually give way to the Divine True and Real Self of you, the self that reside in infinite eternal existence just as the Real and Divine True universe does.

So the part of you that is in the self of your body life, it is that part of yourself that is desirous of experiencing the Greater Good by the physical action of your body life self.

The Greater Good is that Divine action that cause salvation to be of your Mind, because it is the Mind of your body life that has been deceived and taken control of in life and it is your Divine mind that is being held captive in the prism of your Body life.

It is your Divine Mind that need to be set free and not your Soul, which is the very essence of your body life, it being the Divine Energy that serve to be your inert ethereal self, the self that is beyond being captured by the physical action of your profane mind body life activities.

The Mind is that attribute of the Soul and the soul is the God that dwells within your body life, the soul being the Divine Intelligent Energy that causes the body locomotion to take place, which is revealed by the action of your body life.

Only by the Greater Good of your body life expression, is that which will cause you to know the Divine value of Freedom and independence from evil.

You must seek Justice during the time of your body life living and that is what will cause your body life to experience the peace and Joy of life action.

Your body life action must be of those principles of the greater good, it all must happen by the present practice of living Divinely virtuous and that will cause you to have knowledge of self, control of thought, patience, temperance, fortitude, acknowledgement of those with Divine Wisdom, and with the ability to Divinely teach those divine virtuous principles.

Being in such a mental divine order can cause you to know of your ability to cause that which will be revealed inside of yourself, which will have you to be with an awareness of the esoteric and alchemy Divine happening that reveal you being with the experience of your Divine Spirituality.

It is your divine spirituality that is expressed in a way that reveal the mental salvation of your mind, which is the expression of the mental energy that guide your body life in the way it is being lived and expressed by your body action, it being such an action that display your Spirituality and it is whether it be divine or profanely expressed.

The effort to obtain the Greater Good in Life became the responsibility of mankind after the fall of the Divine Beings, and it became a requirement of life if your life is to experience justice, peace, and joy again on earth.

Because as it is in Heaven (eternal Infinity) is not as it is on earth, now that the fall of the Divine Being has occurred, and now you must strive to make it so again by striving to become again the Divine Being of character whose body life living is to enjoy the greater good in spirit that life is entitle to enjoy.

Life requires that your attitude and behavior to be impeccable when displaying and expressing the Divine spirit of your body life.

HEAVEN AND HELL:

Based on the religious teaching about heaven and hell and the place it is described to be, well, it is not as so described to be and yes there is no religious heaven and hell that is applicable to your life, since life is for the body and the body life way of living is what reveal the quality of your mind.

Then it is the mind that create heaven and hell to be just a state of your mind belief that is caused by the lack of ability to be in control of the way that you choose to use your mind, in the performance of it guiding your body life to Think and perform.

After the fall of the Divine Beings and now that you have a choice in life to make, which was not needed for you to make at the Time when life was lived Divinely,

It was the fall of the Divine Being is what caused you to either believe or to Rationally Think your way about the meaning and purpose of your body life and which mental act you are to choose to use in order to guide your body life.

The choices you now make in life today is what now determine the quality of living that your body life will experience, over the course of your body life way of living, and the type of life you live, is now determine by the state and quality of your mind thoughts.

The quest to enter into heaven is now what give you the motivation to live in pursuit of you wanting to go to heaven, as if it is a physical place in the sky, it being the space where all objects play out their movement in the presence of each other, far and near.

The cause for Heaven to be believed to be real, is caused by a rigorous religious belief system that was created by mankind, men who have formed and organized themselves into an oligarchy in an effort to act in defiance to the natural order of all things that have cause for being.

There are men in power today with a profane spirit, they now have an insatiable urge to dominate and control all things that are part of the world and they are the Beings who are in control of your mind, you who have became a part of the world today.

Life extend no further than your body life and its domain of life is in the physical state of all things that move and is propelled by the energy that is on the outside as well as inside of the physical objects and they have an ability to change in appearance from the appearance that the objects originally were while in their physical state of being, the objects now in action in the universe.

Heaven is a fixture based on the fiction of illusion residing in the mind of a profane mind, its concept coming from the few who now present to you their own sense of reality that is now formed by people with a profane mind and have lost their divinity.

They are Beings whose original state of being has been transformed to become Human Beings with a profane mind.

Hell on the other side of the equation of life religious destiny, is a place of residence deep in the earth and hell imply that if you have not been obedient to God commandments you will linger in a state of forever pain and damnation, which is the same act of implication by its counter part, heaven, but more peaceful than hell is told to be.

Hell being no more than a fixture created by a profane mind to bring fear into your mind and it being a place that is the fiction of an illusion being portrayed as a real place located inside of the earth, it being a bottomless pit formed to be by the mind ability to believe what is not Divinely true and real, but in religion, hell is taught to be true and real and such a requirement of the mind is what cause you to believe in Heaven and Hell, and only a mind that is not functioning divinely is capable of such a religious belief about Hell.

Hell has no place in the mind that is in pursuit of guiding your body life in an effort to experience the greater good in life way of living, and hell must be dismissed and accepted for what it is, which is a figment of your religious mind imagination.

Such an imagination is used to conjure up fear in your mind for religious purposes and that is to have an oligarchy of evil Beings of mankind controlling your mind, guiding it in the way you are to believe about events that occur in your life.

All such a belief about heaven and hell is based upon religious teaching that cause you to Believe in hell when such a belief is a sign that you are not in control of your mind, and it is the mind that you must be in control of again, today.

So, if you are ever again to master the virtues that reveal your Divinity which is the only way that you will be able to experience your Divine Spirituality, an act of mind qualified to take you into its outer limits and into the abyss of your Divine Reality, then you must by divine interaction with the inner self, master the knowledge of self.

The way to master knowledge of self is by studying the action of the universe which require you to Think with a mind of your own chosen action and that is what will allow you to enter the dimension where Divine Truth reside in an inert infinite state of unending action.

It is not an easy task to master the knowledge of self because it require a mind of Divine quality and virtues of patience and endurance that compliment life and only then you will come to know and understand the physical and nonphysical action of both universe.

You will gain such knowledge by having self discipline and mastering the art of comparative reasoning, a way of thinking that will have you to form a rational conclusion about things that you observe and have come to know about and not what somebody else tell you to believe about those things that confront your life and by the use of such mind control it will have you to be in confidence with your self. .

The reason you must come back into the knowledge of self is to bring self worth to your self and that will bring you to understand how significant to the universe that you are, because without knowledge and understanding, it will prove that you have not mastered living a life of virtue which cause your way of life to be that of the divine motion of the universe, both of the universes of which you occupy.

Of the two universe one is infinite and the other is physical, the infinite universe being the eternal space darkness and it being the Holiest of Holy place in which the Divine Essence (GOD) inertly reside.

After the fall of the Divine Being, the purpose of life is to bring salvation back to your Mind, it being the process of your body life that is responsible for guiding your life action and it being an action that will reveal the quality of your Spirituality.

HATE:

In life you are judged by the quality of your character which reveal its content when it is that of a greater good or a lesser evil, either way; it all is taking place by the action of your mind.

Hate can be a Divine virtue or it can cause the action of evil, it all depend the way it appear coming from your body life action, because you see, it is a Divine virtue to hate evil ways and action that reveal the content and quality of your character, which reveal the quality of the mind that is guiding your life action.

Hate is just another part of your mind expression, it has nothing to do with religion, it has all to do with your body life perception, and hate become a part of your life expression based upon how you are relating to all of that which you are perceiving that is coming from those events that are having an effect in your life living condition.

Hating can be an elevating aspect of your life action or it can serve as a hindrance to your life Divine elevation, it all depend on the character and quality of the hating.

In your Divine state of mind, you are obligated to hate all of those things that serve as a hindrance to your body life that prevent you from being able to experience the greater good in life.

Therefore, to pretend not to hate will knock you off of your life natural equilibrium, because you see, you are being dishonest to your mind instruction when your life is exposed to acts of evil against you and you make claim to love everybody while being in such a living miserable predicament.

So the fact that there is the emotion of hate, it assure there being the emotional principal of what we call love and it is all in keeping with the natural law of opposites.

All that happens in your life really mean that at the end of the end of each day and night, all that have happened that had a direct effect upon your life did and do cause such an action of expression by you that reveal the state of mind that is causing you to be expressive in your life.

So it is those events that are happening in your body life is what is affecting your life way that you are living, be it in an acceptable or an unacceptable to you.

Each way, what is happening in your life is effective in affecting your body life way of living and such life emotional expressions are no more than a display of your state of mind thoughts.

Our senses are of value to our body life based upon the state of our mind and it is our mind that is most important to our body life, so it is our mind that qualify us to be emotional responsive to the things that occur in our life.

So yes, it is a Divine virtue to hate that which prevents life from experiencing the greater good for your self.

LOVE:

Based upon the principals and law of opposites of the universe, you can not Love without having the option to hate when living in an evil environment and love is of no greater virtue than hate, when applied and expressed divinely.

The two, love and hate is no more than an emotional expression and is not mutual exclusive, which is generated by the mind, as it is evaluating events that are occurring in your life that is reflecting the value and action of your body life sense of perception.

So, what does it imply when it is said that you are either being loving or mean and hateful toward someone, is not the two just an expression of your mind sprit about a situation that is occurring and is affecting your life and is having an effect in your life in an acceptable or unacceptable way?

Is it not natural for you to respond indicating how your senses are signaling to your mind that which the senses are experiencing and isn't it your mind that is instructing what your response should and will be in any given situation that is being revealed by your sense action that is affecting how your life is to respond in either a dramatic or calm fashion, depending on the gravity of the situation?

What do we mean when we say it is better to love than to hate, other than it being an opinion which has been established and is based upon a religious belief and it all is tied to the Heaven and Hell dynamics of a religious doctrine, it being nothing concretely verifiable, just a belief based upon a fictional illusion that does more harm to your life than good.

Such a belief system based upon religious dogma is what such a belief has the power to prevent you from experiencing the greater good in life, which include Love having an option to divinely hate.

Did I not inform you that this is a book that will be revealing to you the quality of information that does not correspond nor conform to that which has been taught to you and will not be politically and religiously correct as you have been indoctrinated to believe about life?

This is a book that will call your attention to those things that will assist you in how you can experience the greater good in your life living as well as the highest order of your Divine Spirituality.

So, what you do not need to do is to read this book with a challenging spirit, because if you have at this point, then you have missed the dignity and Divinity of this book, which is to inform you of the path you must take in order to experience your Divine Spirituality.

Love is a mental expression interlocked with your sensual perceived attraction, which cause you to have a body stimulated emotional experience caused by the mind and it being no more than energy in action, revealing the quality of your mind which is sending out from you a spiritual action.

Your spirit being that which is expressed by your body action with the body sometimes revealing an emotion caused by the sense to mind interaction which we refer to as love and / or hate, joy and sadness, pain, calmness, all depending upon the emotional state of the moment.

Your life journey which is caused by your sense to mind spiritual expression by your body life living action van be that which display the emotion of a life that is enjoying the greater good in your life expression or a greater disappointment in your life living expression.

It all depend on the nature and quality of virtues that are being revealed by your spiritual expression with your body life involved pursuit, it being to experience the greater good for your life living condition .

Since the fall from your divine state of the Being that you once were a party to, your body life challenges have been exploded with confusion, lies, and deceit, causing you to not know the Divine nature of yourselves.

That what is having you to believe that the experience of the greater good in life is an unattainable goal and that it is by nature design that we are to be a Being in pursuit of a life that extends beyond this body life.

Such is the religious belief that serves as a hindrance to prevent you from experiencing the greater good in this life, which is only for the body, after it, there is no more life to be experienced in the body physical.

So it is in your body life that is now, that you should be depended upon, knowing that you have the ability to bring salvation back to your mind again, so that your life can experience the greater good in this life and none other here after.

MORALITY:

I WILL END THE CONCLUSION with what I WOULD LIKE FOR THE READER TO EXPERIENCE AFTER READING THIS BOOK.

When dealing with your Divine Spirituality, nothing is more paramount to verify such a Divine Life way of living than the morals you display in the way you live your life.

So I guess the question become, what do we mean about morals and is there a difference in being moral in our lives decision making, which is to reflect how we Think and act toward others.

Do we have to strive to be moralistic, which is more of being self serving to get the attention of others than to live by a set of life principles you have set for yourselves?

The question is, will you cause your self to be of service that will cause you to be able to experience the Greater Good of others as well as for your selves?

There is no Divine benefit to be gained by being moralistic as oppose to being one with a moral character, you must come to understand that there is nothing alchemic about morality, because it take a conscious concerted effort to be a person of a moral Divine Spirit.

Such a spirit could be expressed by a single person, by a group, or by a government that is in full action of assisting others for the sake to fulfill the need of others and for recognizing a wrong done, by offending divine principles of others.

Being Moral, is having a set of standards that are adopted by you and will only serve to bring about the Greater Good by you to your self and to others.

So, to bring salvation to the life living condition to those people whose living condition is of a substandard living condition in relationship to the living norm of a society of which you are a member of, there must be the expression of a Divine Spirituality by us all.

So to be moral is to be Divine and to be moralistic is to be vainly and selfishly pretentious in your life living action, so being moralistic will prevent you from being divinely spiritual.

Being moral has nothing to do with being right or wrong or good or bad, such is a moralistic status, but to be a moral Being, it mean you must be a Divine Being and it is Divinity that transcend being moralistic, because in being Divine you live a life that is in complete Harmony, Order, and Balance, a Mind that reflect your Divine Spirituality.

A Divine Spirit reflect an attitude and behavior that is expressed toward others, and is done by your Divine Will to do Divinely good toward others in life.

Your body life should be lived to assist others when in need or not in need, because such a life expression is not based upon expectation of reward or condemnation for your action, it is done because of your Divine compassion toward others in life.

SUMMARY:

1. Divine Essence

In this book is revealed to you what the Divine Essence (GOD) is and not who "HE IS", this book share with you information about the Divine Essence that will have you to know that "GOD" is not of a gender physical presence, as you and I.

The Divine Essence is the alchemy presence that cause the Divine Energy To Be and NOT TO BE, it is inside of the physical and not of the physical, the Divine Essence is in the Energy that cause all things physical and is not physical TO BE, and NOT TO BE.

So in order to read to understand this book about your Divine Spirituality you must be able to grasp what this book has revealed to you about the Divine Essence and about its attributes, and your body life, and the self of you that is of the body, and is out of your physical body.

The Divine Essence is what give Soul to the Universe and all of its parts that are seen and not seen, IT is the Essence of the Energy that cause the space Time continuum To Be.

The Divine Essence is what cause you to be, but is not in the business of causing you to believe how to be, when expressing your self in your body life.

In life there come with it a Will to act and should not be based upon the influence coming from others that are causing the choices you make in life.

So what your will is to be, and the choices you make for your life, it should be for you alone to make.

The Divine Essence is of the Energy of all things that moves in the inertness of its existence and yet do not move because of its eternal infiniteness.

The Divine Essence require nothing from all that It has caused physically "TO BE" and "NOT TO BE", but is what It Is To Be To All Things.

So the body life which the Divine Essence give to you, it is that life that require much and is obtained in life by you, so what ever is obtained for your life by you, is determined by the nature and quality of your spirituality.

Your Spirituality being the attitude and behavior that must be Divine in order to know what it is that is required of your self and not for the Divine Essence.

The Divine Essence, (GOD) it does not require anything from you and it is in need of nothing from you, yet has caused you To Be.

It is the greater good that cause life to be sacred and it is that good that bring salvation to the mind, because only through such a Divine mind, the greater good is experienced in life, and that Greater Good is the Divine Essence that dwell within the energy that cause your mind to be an active part of your body life.

The Divine Essence (GOD) promise you nothing, nor does it command anything from you, the life you live is the life that is guided by your mind and that is what the Divine Essence has allowed to be a part of your body life economy.

So now, after our fall from being the life living of a Divine Being, the fall is what have caused you to lose all knowledge of thyself.

So we now spend our life in an attempt to know the Divine Essence (GOD) when in fact you do not know thyself, and it is such a lack of knowledge that have you to believe in fantasies about the Divine Essence, the GODLY ENERGY, which is not the cause of the way the world is now putting on such a display of a spirit that is no longer the expression of a Divine mind.

So, the Divine Essence do not promise you a place in Heaven nor in Hell, It just give you the opportunity to create such a body life living for yourselves.

Therefore now you allow your life to be based upon the way you have come to be persuaded to believe about the Soul of your body life, a should that is not in need of being saved, it is your life that is in such a need..

It is not the Soul that is in need of being saved and it is in fact that which cause your Mind thought process and it is the mind ability to think Divinely that is in need of being saved, a process if the mind is Divine will qualify you to know what GOD Is and Is Not, which is Energy of the Divine Essence, and it is the Divine Intelligence that has no beginning or ending or a need to be saved.

The alchemy Divine Essence is the God that is Divine Intelligence, the Energy that give life to its finished product life, it being all that is of the physical universe.

2. UNIVERSE

There are two universe, one is physical and the other is nonphysical, yet the two are connected by the fact of their presence, one coming forth from the other verifying each to be of intimate relationship with the other, as one is the cause for the other To Be and Not To Be.

When dealing with the universe you must come to know the infinite and finite of the two, one being the cause for the continuous motion of the other, the infinite always being the cause for the finite universe.

The finite universe that consist of the stars and planets and since all things physical having a meaning and purpose for being and each of its part affect the other as all that Be and Not Be, inside of it all does the Divine Essence reside.

The physical universe reveal the presence of the immeasurable power of the nonphysical universe and it is the physical universe through which the cavities (Black Holes) revealing an action that is caused by the presence of the infinite universe, it being the night of eternity, that which reveal and verify the presence and the power of the nonphysical universe, as it has been stated in this book.

So the claim of Black Holes are a mischaracterization of the fact concerning the everlasting universe, because infinity can not be penetrated to reveal a hole in its eternal Black Spatial Body and it is such a body that is a verification to be space, which has no boundaries.

The infinite eternal universe is the alchemical action that produces continuously the physical universe and it being the universe that consists of stars and planets and the elements of life.

The physical universe is given to be with life that is caused by the nonphysical universe and it being the Ethereal Eternal Infinite Darkness serving as a verification of the presence of GOD.

It is that infinite darkness that has come to be considered by the coming of Human Beings, to be a representation of evil and is also the way you now identify life unacceptable events that cause suffering to come to your body life living.

Anything Black is considered to be Bad Luck, which is a deceived belief that have you to believe that anything that happen in your life that is unacceptable to your life, the reason being because there is a dark cloud over your head that is the cause for those unacceptable events to be effecting your life and that is what causing you to be competitive in life instead of being cooperative in life with each other.

The things we have been taught to believe that are without facts to verify what you believe is true, is immeasurable and yet we remain a victim of such fictional belief about things that we know nothing about.

The Universe is the verifying Intelligence of the Divine Essence of the God Energy, that which is of no Gender

Identity, but is the producer of the principles that are different and opposite to each other and those principles are the objects that make up to be the physical universe, which is in motion, which serve to be the evidence of life in action.

3. RELIGION

Such an institution as religion is the reason why you have a belief about God, and it is that institution that was constructed by people calling themselves no longer Divine Beings but now has come to be Human Kind of a Being.

It is religion that introduced a method of believing about God that caused you to no longer know about the Divine Essence. (GOD)

Religion is a creation by the Human Being, and Divine Spiritual awareness come from the knowledge of the Divine Essence and not from religion.

Religion is that which has its God to send out Commands to you and religion is the creator of Heaven and Hell, a fantasy of illusion, as been depicted by the Human Being religion.

All religion is of the Human Being and it is the Human Being that created the characters and terms, such as Devil, Satan, Lucifer, and religion claim to be the Daughter and Son of them all, the moment you came to believe that never upon this earth or any place else in the Universe, you were ever perfect in your body life living.

It is religion that now causes you to confess to be born in Sin and is shaped in inequity, the twin of Evil action.

Religion represent the fall of the Divine Beings, those whose Divinity has dissolved into becoming a Human Being and now believe in a created God that require for you to be shrouded in belief, faith, and hope, based upon a foundation of wishful uncertainty.

There is a difference in Religious Spirituality and Divine Spirituality, one is based upon belief and the other is of Divine Knowledge, and all is taking place in the processes of your mind and it is the quality of your mind that determine the quality of the religious God, as well as your Divine Spirituality.

To be religious does not mean that you are divinely spiritual, religion teaches you to believe about the fallibility of the Human Being and the theology of Divine Spirituality Reveal the elevation of the Divine Being.

Religion teach not to be perfect and Divinity reveal your need to become your perfection, religion is physical and Divinity is Spiritual, religion is about the body and Spirituality is about the body mind.

Religious Spirituality and Divine Spirituality are diametrically oppose to each other body life action, both being a action of the mind process, and that is why the

257

quality of your mind is utterly important to the way your body life will be guided to live and relate to the Divine Essence and / or to the God of your Religion.

Religion serves to be a detriment to your Divine Spirituality because religion is physically deceptive and Divine Spirituality is alchemically ethereally real and is revealed by your body life action.

4. FEAR

Fear is an emotion that control the body life and can cause you to do things you would not ordinarily do in your body life, it cause you to believe in things that you know nothing about and your body life suffers because of your body life uncertainties about those things that you allow to become a part of your way of believing about them.

Anything that give you cause for your life to be guided by fear, serve as a sign of it not being divine in its action and it is fear that disrupt the Divine order in which your life should be revolving.

Fear of the unknown is a fear of the Divine Essence, (GOD) you indicate fear in a belief in God but the Divine Essence is not to be feared and without fear is what indicate you have knowledge with understanding about the Divine Energy, that which is of the Divine Essence.

Fear come to the weak of mind and it is claimed to have come with life, but it is allowed to be a part of your life emotion because of your religious fear and has its root in what you have been told to believe about life involvements that cause you to be afraid in life.

It is all about what you know, is what prevent life from having the emotion of fear, but it is because of your religious belief that fear is serving as evidence of your discomfort with your body life living condition that is based upon fear.

All that you do not know serve as fuel that bring on fear and the emotion of self destruction and that is what cause you to have a psychological imbalance in your life.

Fear is the cause for you being no longer in control of your Divine Mind, the mind that qualify you to be able to reason rationally and logically about all those things that come to be a part of your body life and is what cause your life living condition.

Fear is an enemy to life when not divine and Divine Wisdom is the protector of your body life, because to fear is to believe, and where there is doubt, your life become an action motivated by fear and not Divine knowledge with understanding of those events that confront your body life.

5. DEATH

What is death other than an action that bring to close the illusion of the physical body life action, AND There Has Been Given The Wrong Impression That Death RELATIONSHIP Is To Life.

Death is a part of life and is not to be feared, death is what allow your body life to be alive, because without the presence of death in your life, then your life cease to be.

By the absent of death to your life your life cease to be, but because of the presence of death to your body life, that is what cause your body life to be in motion.

So death is the phenomena dynamic that is necessary to the body life being alive, yet you have been taught to fear death and to accept it to be an enemy to your body life, but when in the Divine scheme of things, death presence is what keep your body life to be in motion.

The moment death detach away from your body life, your body life cease to be in motion and it is motion that verify life and without motion death is no longer present in your body life and your body began the process of what we call decomposition, fading back into the elements that cause your body life physical To Be.

Death is not when it is no longer a part of your body life action, it is when death is inactive in your body life that cause your body life to be in motion, so death is what cause life To Be and life is to be a body with motion, (Life) as long as death is present in your life .

I know that this information about death relationship to life may seem far fetch for you to comprehend, not alone accept, but didn't I inform you at the beginning of this book that it is not a book that conform to your established beliefs, but it will expose you to revelation that contradict the way you have been taught to believe and not know about your body life happenings?

This book is about Divine Truth about thyself, which require you to be of your Divine Spirituality, because Divine Truth is reasonable and rational in disseminating information that you are capable of taking to a logical conclusion about the topic being discussed.

So when dealing with death you must deal with life and vice versus, because the two can not be without the other in the body life.

Life is to death as death is to life, so again, you can not have one without the other being present in life, so Life is for the body and is not beyond the body life, where there is no body life, only the state of eternal infinite existence, not even death reside in the dimension of existence, the dimension where the body life does not dwell.

So there is no life after death, which mean that you should live to enjoy the Greater Good while of life, so that your body life will be able to experience now, today, and taking no belief about tomorrow, because life and death is about yesterday and today.

6. SOUL

So much has been said about what is referred to as the Soul, so in this book it has been revealed that the Soul is the essence that cause your body to be alive and it is the soul that is not in need of being saved, your soul is your body source of Divine Energy that give your body motion. (LIFE)

It is the Mind process that has been attacked and has been given cause to function below its capacity to divinely reason, and it is an irrational mind that has no logic in its ability to reason, using Divine Thought.

So what happen, you end up believing everything that is told to you regardless of how irrational the profane reasoning may be.

The soul seek not a place in heaven nor in hell, it provide to your body a life you are to live to the greater good that is based upon the choices you make that will and does affect your life, and anything less put you in the want to believe that it is your soul that is in want of being saved and not your mind, and want is a very irrational selfish mental act.

The soul is the equivalent to that which you refer to as the pituitary gland, the energy source that feed the body the energy of life, but the quality of that life is left entirely up to you.

The soul serve as the kundalini, which is energy points of the body that provide performance of the body life in a way that the body life become a mental conscious Being, you with energy attributes that can cause transformation of the body life performance, displaying a sign of its Mind divine intelligence or ignorance masquerading as intelligence. The soul serves as the central theme in your body, there to give it motion. (LIFE)

7. MIND-HEART

The mind in all practical purpose is what gives what you refer to as the heart, its meaning and purpose to appear to be what it is not to the body life action.

To describe the interaction between the sense and mind is to describe an ethereal action that is taking place inside of the body life performance, which is what being called love and devotion coming from the heart, in this case the mind.

So when describing the sensation that is being revealed by the action of the mind, which is causing the body sensual experience, you end up describing such an act that is claimed to be a performance of the "heart" but is of the mind, and it is that experience that give off a euphoric divine expressed feeling that is being expressed by the body.

It is that body pleasing euphoric experience that is being caused by a display of the action between the sense mind interaction that can be pleasing to you, or it can be antagonizing and discomforting to you, either way, you end up describing such a body life experience as being an action caused by the heart, which is no more than an action of the mind mental expression generated by the soul of your body essence, the kundalini (energy) being the source of the central points of the body nerve points which give to your body a mental sensation that the body life is experiencing and is being caused by the mind.

Sensational life experiences come from the energy that allow the mind to guide the body in the way it express its self and by the mind having such an effect on the body, it cause your body to be able to express those feelings of sensation we call love and hate, such is the way that we do in life.

It is the mind guiding the body that causes it to act in different ways of spiritual expression, we are describing such action as being an act of the heart.

It is not the organ heart, but an organic mind felt expressed experience, as you describe your feelings with an indication that you are having feelings of love or hate, meaning that there is that feeling full of pleasure or dissatisfaction.

That which is referred to as the heart is no more than the mind action, expressed in a spirit of sensual emotions, displayed by the body life performance.

8. MEDITATION

Meditation is a ritual used to help you move mentally from the conscious to the subconscious level to your inner self dimension.

Meditation is used to enter into deeper dimensions of the not mental inner self, it is an actual process that give off an alchemy experience that is beyond the conscious level, the level which put you in contact with the intuitiveness of your inner self, that is the level that will take you beyond the boundaries of your mind action, an action that can be experienced with or without the method of meditation.

Meditation is about you being in search for a deeper meaning to your life and to experience life past and present activity, things that took place in your past life action, and now is taking place in your present life action in the physical universe.

Such awareness can come to you on the conscious and subconscious level of your mind and beyond into the intuitive dimension of your inner self.

But that which is being intuitively revealed come without the mind experience about your past and present lives which are present in your DNA,

So it is about the intuitive revelation that reveals to you the inert ethereal activity that is present in the eternal infinite nonphysical universe.

Meditation is used to calm the mind activity and to bring solace to the body life mind, it is used to put you into the various energy centers of your body life and that can only be done in a Divine spiritual state of meditation, regardless of how you are performing in life on the conscious level.

You can become divinely spiritual in the act of meditation; the requirement being to those who participate in such a mental process, is the same that require a spiritual discipline.

So the information you receive from your meditation and how you use that information in your body life action is a responsibility that is yours alone and you will receive the consequence from your body life action.

Meditation prove to you just how versatile and powerful the mind is and can be, so with a Divine mind used in unity with others whose thoughtful goal is the same, then such a mental unity can in fact cause that goal to be attained.

So, that is why the oligarchy of evil Human Beings are always busy at conditioning your mind what to believe and how to believe about things that your body life is being confronted with in the world, which has an effect on how you live your body life.

Meditation is an action provided by the soul that help you to gain divinity for your body life and it really does matter in what state of mind you are in when you practice the ritual of meditation, because it is all about the mind and as it has been stated in this book, there is nothing that gets by the Mind on the physical conscious level.

A divine mind is required to reach an uncontrolled level out of your mind, meaning all of your meditative effort must be in harmony, order, and balance with the soul, and with such a Divine spirit, your journey should be one that bring you to a state of deep out consciousness.

Such deep meditation will take you out of the state of consciousness and into the inner dimension of intuitive awareness, causing you to experience the alchemic and esoteric action that is revealed to you information which is not coming from the mind.

9. GOD, SPIRIT, MOTION, REINCARNATION

God, Spirit, Motion, Reincarnation, these inert ethereal principals are the alchemy esoteric mysteries that the body life is curious about and is your hunger to believe about what has been told to you.

Some of you have gotten to know about those things concerning the Divine truth and reality about those entities that others have caused chills of fear in you or to be happy about things that are told to you about those entities.

God, Spirit, Motion, Reincarnation, these are all a part of your body life expressed concerns and all of them are made to be an assured part of your life curiosity.

When dealing with the God, Spirit, and Motion, which is an expressed act of your body life belief system, it is common to express your belief / thoughts concerning those entities and you claim a position of whether or not you receive to perceive each of them to be true and real by you, such become an act of pretending through belief.

Take for instance the entity God and those who take a position to either be an atheist or an agnostic, such a position has no play in your body life that hold to be creditable.

Because of the fact that you are taking such a position about the Divine Essence, (GOD) is fact enough that prove what you are able to claim not to be real and true, is real and true.

So those who claim that there is no God or that they hold no opinion either way about God reality, you do so in words only, while the mere fact of your body life contradict such a doubtful claim about God being not real and true, is your body life.

God, spirit, and motion, is one in action and many in various levels of expression, the God Essence have numerous attributes that verify its existence, it is those Divine entities are the reason why you are in motion and is capable of spiritual expression, but when it come to reincarnation, it become another matter that is entirely based on belief.

When dealing with reincarnation what immediately come to mind is that your body life is being recycle, believing you might not come back in life in the form that you left here with but the life memory system remain intact in its come back approach, which is one belief about reincarnation.

The other belief about reincarnation is that as you left here through the corridor of death, you will return again the same way that you left and that is with memory intact but with a new body.

The Divine Essence need not to be in the recycle business, so I am of the mind that it is given to life once to die but to the soul that caused that life to be, it dwell in eternal existence as does the Divine Essence, it being the eternal infinite intelligence over us all.

The Divine Essence is without ceasing and is in a continued process of having all things to be in a motion of coming and going, and it is the cause for all things physical and not physical to be and those physical bodies is what constitute the physical universe.

Reincarnation is religious teaching with a promise, and is not a fact of Divine Truth and Reality, which make no promise to all that is a part of the process of God action.

So the spirit and motion of life is in a constant coming and going, and is given only once to be, and eternally not To Be, it is the physical Body Life I speak of.

10. DIVINE SPIRITUALITY SEXUALITY

As has been so stated, there is Divine Spiritual sexuality and there is what we refer to as physical sexuality, each action take place in and by the body life.

There is sexual intimate encounter and there is Divine Spiritual intimate encounter, and there is Divine sexual personality, and there is profane sexual personality, all such action summing up the sexual character of the body life and with an indication of the sexual gender involved.

Beings who are of a Divine Spiritual sexuality, present such a beauty of the body life that is beyond comparison, because the personality and character of your gender action is well within the bounds of Harmony, Order, And Balance.

That is what is indicated by the expression of your attitudinal behavior, it being your outward spiritual appearance and is of such neatness that says a lot about the quality of mind that guides your body life.

 It is that Divine quality of mind, when engaged on all levels of sexual encounter, cause an ecstasy euphoria to be expressly enjoyed by the body life that is under the control by your mind action.

A profane sexuality is guided by a spirit of irresponsibility, self neglect, and lust driven; such an action of the body life is guided by a mind with a spiritual expression of disrespect, a mind full of profanity and not Divinity.

Divine Spiritual Sexuality is an expression of the mind, while profane spiritual sexuality is an expression of the senses dominating the mind, each having their place in the body life action that is having a dynamic relationship between the gender opposites.

Need I say that the gift of divine quality goes to those whose sexuality is divinely spiritual grounded, coming from A Divine Mind?

11. CHANGE

All change is not good change and the change that come to your life is caused by evil men, that is not good change and neither is such change natural to your body life experience.

When living a Divine Spiritual life, that life is being lived by nature time and action, it is that kind of life change you should be living and that type of change that come to your body life is good change, because it is change caused by the guidance of your Divine mind and not the mind of evil Beings of human quality.

Divine change is a natural characteristic of the physical Universe, everything is based upon a continued action of coming and going, being and not being, such action being an attribute of change.

Change can take you from living a Divine Life to living a profane life, so being constant in your natural change is a Divine good thing which is the goal of all divine intelligent life form that is of an anthropomorphous nature.

When living a profane body life such living condition is in a caste class of vain envy, ego, and jealousy, the trinity of spiritual evil, a change in your body life living that is not good, and the body life natural objective should be to experience the greater good for your life living condition.

Change is based upon both spiritual and physical action, the former is caused by the quality of your mind action and the latter is caused by your physical action, both that expresses the nature of your spirituality.

In life we seek change in accordance to our body life living condition, other wise the change that is sure to come to our body life without you seeking for such a change, that is what you call the aging process and it begin with you from conception to death.

AUTHOR NOTE:

To the reader I must say that my objective in writing this book is to deal with a few of the topics that you might be curious about and to do so without boring you with the same regimented established explanation of such topics.

I have touched upon in this book many of such topics, but the most important thing in this book is to get you to know that in your body life living and being confronted with the myriads of events that effect your body life, all that you do most time is reacting to things in life.

That is what become the cause and affect that affect your body life living condition, and all of those things do in fact passes through the channel of your mind.

So in your body life, the objective should be to control your own mind thoughts, other wise, you become the property of someone else thoughts.

You may contact the author for speaking engagement; lecturing and or questions you might have which pertain to the content in this book at, o_akkebala2002@yahoo. com and you will be given a number you can call.

THIS IS THE BEGINNING OF THE END TO ALL OF THE LIES THAT IS TOLD ABOUT GOD, HEAVEN, HELL, AND LIFE.

THANK YOU

THE AUTHOR

OSIRIS AKKEBALA

After Thoughts

LIFE

Here In This Life There Is Nothing New, Beyond Life There Is nothing Old

There is much today that we take for granted about Life and yet we have become a people that move so fast until we have lost the virtue of patience and it is because of that handicap, which we have in our lives, we miss out from knowing the essential things about Life, not my life or your life but Life as the general to all moving objects in space, affected by Time.

Life in and of its independent action, is Motion Divine, Moving in Harmony, Order, and Balance, in the Infinite darkness of Space, creating Time, because in actuality, Time is Motion and Life is the result there from.

So it is Divine to know that when it is about Life action, there is nothing New that is govern by the actionable Divine Energy that is generated by the Sun action, but when the attention is about Life in and of its Motion, independent of its attributes, which is action and motion that is expressed through your body life living.

Such a physical interaction with life, is what give cause for there to be nothing that is New in Action and motion, that verify the physical result that come from Life action and motion, generated by the life of the Sun. (Stars)

So regarding Life, there is nothing New that occur by the body, but do occur in the body life of your Being, change take place caused by the events that happen in your life, and those events are separate and apart from your life, as they become a part of your life experiences, as those events are having an affect upon the body Life, which is not a part of your Divine existence.

Life is of a continue physical cycle, changing, but is always the same, nothing new in the actionable motion which is life.

The life cycle never change from start to finish, causing not the body life living, but does cause the actionable motion of life to be the Divine representative of Infinity, and it is that Divine phenomena that exceed the physical aspect of your body life and is the Divine representative of Existence, that which exceed the gravity of Life and is not subject to Change.

So life is amenable to Action, Motion, and Change, they are kindred principle action that verify the oneness of Life actionable motion, the life motion that verify the continuum of the Linear action of life, from Start to finish.

It is only Divine Existence that never grows old and never is subject to change, always in action from start to start and is the entity that is of the Essence that cause there to be nothing in Life that is New.

Only existence never changes and is not subject to a start and finish cycle, nor is it subject to Time in its existence, it reside beyond life, in an inert perpetual actionable motion, where existence and Time is one and the same.

It is in the body life living action, there it is, creating Time, of which it is subject to, revolving in the Divine Infinite Space, that Divine Black Cover where therein is intrinsic the no ending presence of Divine existence, there, without being expose to having a beginning nor an ending, as it reside within the Divine Dark cover of the Divine Existence, that which is never New nor grow Old in its Divine Existence.

In the experience of Life body living, there is nothing new that happen to life, yet in life there is the experience of growing old, as we call it to be, but in Divine Existence, there is nothing New nor is there the experience of growing old, because in such a Divine Dimension, the inertness in infinity, there is your constant Divine companion, it being the Divine Essence of It All.

DIVINE NATURE OF LIFE AND THE CONFUSION WE HAVE ABOUT LIFE

If Your Belief Is Of established Religion, Then Your Mind Is Not Calibrated To Accept This Which I Am Sharing With You, Beloved.

So Who It Is That Suffer The Fault From Such Divine Revelation, The Foolish Among Us, That Is guided by Ignorant Intelligence.

REINCARNATION

There is a misrepresentation of reincarnation in definition, some people take it to mean the return from death in another form or in the form you died with, not so.

Reincarnation is the embodiment of and the personification of the genetic body of those you are the direct descendant of.

Therefore, you become incarnate with inner personification of your Ancestors, because of your Genetic connection to them, their Genetic code is what you carry and is what cause you to be able to know, see, feel, and communicate with them, as well as with yourself, Mentally and genetically, using the senses as well as the Mind.

Therefore you are the incarnate of your Ancestors and not your Ancestors reincarnation separate from you, thus you have the Divine Action of the Oneness and Continuum of your Ancestors being the reincarnation inside of you, Genetically and not physically.

Therefore, The One Entity being the Divine Essence of all Things Non-physical, become the reincarnation into all thing physical, with the Divine Soul of the Nonphysical being present in all things physical and is Nonphysical, the Divine Soul being the Eternal Everlasting Infinite Energy of Intelligence, the Divine Essence of All Things incarnate.

Because of the Divine Nature of Life, we should Love and Respect All Life, we meaning not just Race Based Life but all Body life with a Conscious Intelligence associated to all Corporeal Anthropomorphous Life Form.

FAMILY LIFE OF MARRIAGE

Here is the problem with what is usually the discussion about the family, marriage, and the feminine - masculine relationship, and based upon our misperception about ourselves and life.

What we all are doing is trying to forge a family relationship structure that will meet our religious wants, trying to do it without paying the price it take to live the type of life you claim to be desirous of to enjoy.

We can talk and discuss and make comparison of ideas about what various Race of people want and not need to do, in order to change the caliber of spirit and belief we now display and express toward each other.

Here you are, claiming that you want to make a change in the condition of your Life, not need but want, while all such talk is as chaff before the wind, if we do not do what come first in constructing the ideal social personal relationship with each other, both intimately mental, and / or Platonic, we will remain expressing the profane spirit which most of the world do.

Now, what do I mean about that, well it is simple, because it does not take a genius to know why it is that we today, behave toward each other as we do, yet here we are sometime discussing ways to change our spirit toward each other, using the Human Being structure and foundation upon which, social behavior rest upon, and that structure consist of a set of so call morals and immoral principles, which is grounded into the foundation of the Human Being Religion, as so conceived by them, Lucifer incarnate.

The problem with the world today is that we are trying to reach spiritual salvation without going through the Fire of Divinely Knowing who we are as a Divine People, a purge of mental cleansing that must take place with all people, before we can begin to know the beauty of Divine relative living.

The perception of marriage is a Human Being construct, with all of the laws and policy that sustain it, here we are discussing all of the problems that infest our Lives as controlled by that institution.

The world has the experience of living under a flawed perception about Feminine, Masculine Relationship, we even have members of the female gender gladly admitting to submitting to their Husband, as if they are in some kind of a slave marriage relationship, which is what the Human Being Marriage system is all about.

The present marriage system is that type of relationship that carry the highest of disrespect the male gender has toward the female gender, it put and keep the female gender in a childish position, always having to ask for and get permission from the husband, depend upon the culture and custom of various societies, before she can do something of her liking or make decision for self, independent of her husband input.

Such is the spirit of a religious believer marriage, and has no relevancy to Divine Relationship, guided by a Divine Mind Thinking ability, with the expression of Divine Spirituality, in term of the Feminine / masculine connection.

In a profane environment you can not imitate Divinity, and in order to construct a Divine Relationship between the female gender and male gender, it will never Divinely materialize within a profane environment.

Today, the majority of World society lives in a profane environment, one that is dominated by the Male gender, and also is controlled by him as well, he having authority over all of our Lives that is of a lower status caused by those who make decision for our lives today.

Yet here we are, many of us and most time, holding vain discussion about such a fallible institution as religious marriage.

To those people who really and Divinely Truly desire to restructure your lives, first thing first, and the first thing you need to admit to and realize, is that, as long as we are functioning without the ability to Divinely Think and Know about our Divine self life, then all else action we take is in pretense.

You can not live Divinely Spiritual in a profane environment and it is the environment that now shape your method of believing, and that is preventing you from Divinely being able to Think and Know what is needed for your life living, in order to become Divinely Spiritual again.

So in order to Divinely change our body life way of living, which we must, and with a desire of having the ability of how we need to Divinely perceive of each other, and do so in relative term and not in equal or unequal term, not until then, will we be qualified to express our Divine Spirit in the presence of others.

In a Divine relationship there is no you lead and I follow, and such an order is based upon your sex gender, no beloved, in such a Divine Gender difference relationship, it is about the order in which you are to each other, that determine the pecking order of advisement, coming from one to the other, absent of vain ego, envy, and jealousy with malice, toward each other.

First seek you to change the quality of your thoughts from being profane to that which must be Divine, and then you will be able to See clearly, that people of a different living status, suffering from abuse and hunger, they are in need of a change from the environment that has caused such a condition to come upon them.

So we must change the quality of spirit that we today express toward each other, a spirit that we today are using to express ourselves, which is profane and is not Divine, a spirit that is dictated by the Human Being Religious doctrine, which we use today as our guide in shaping our Character and Personality, one that is very profane today, and is causing you to, without Divine guidance, attempt to discuss Divine Desires about marriage and relationship, with a profane method of thinking.

LIFE CONDITION AND RESTRICTION

THERE IS NOTHING ABOUT LIFE THAT SHOW THAT LIFE COME WITH CONDITION AND RESTRICTION IN TERM OF THE WAY WE ARE TO LIVE OUR LIVES.

NATURE HAS SO CONSTRUCTED LIFE TO BE ABLE TO BE NATURALLY OBEDIENT TO THE DIVINE UNIVERSAL LAW OF CAUSE AND EFFECT, EXPRESSING AND DISPLAYING A DIVINE SPIRIT TOWARD ALL THINGS THAT IS OF THE DIVINE ESSENCE PERFORMANCE.

So all of the religious and civil laws of the Human Being world, such have been created for purpose to confuse your life and to create condition that effect your life adversely.

Therefore, come the condition of confusion and life believing condemnation, enacted by the Human Being Religion and Civil Law, which has been so constructed for purpose to confuse your Life and to control your Body Life way of using your Mind, which the Human Being fill with contradictions, Lies, and deceptive belief.

It is the Human Being Mind that becomes a condition that causes you to believe in all that a Profane institutions, WILL HAVE YOU TO BELIEVE ABOUT YOUR LIFE.

Such a belief system condition your mind to accept life and not to Divinely live your life, claiming that such a way is being God way of doing things, in regard to your Life, leading you to believe that such a Natural Divine phenomena, Life, come with conditions and Commands straight out of the mouth of God, the God of man.

A God that is not how man has introduced God to be, which is not.

What Ignorant Intelligence that now guides the belief of a once Divine World, Universal in Nature and Divine by the Divine physical action of Nature Life?

What is Life other than the Divine Universality of Motion in Action, connected to the Eternal Infinite universe technology, which represent the action of the Divine Essence, It which in your Life Body, does reside the Winding Ladder of your Genetic verification of Winding Relationship of Divine Truth and Reality, encoded within the Dark Perfection of the Divine Essence, Its Action being Infinite and Precise in Its Presentation Of Life, which is Divine Action in Motion, interacting in Harmony, Order, And Balance with the Divine Infinite Intelligence that form and Reveal all things that come from Its Action in an Intelligent Design.

Meaning that the Divinity of Life is the Evidence of a Divine Essence presenting an Intelligent Design with an Action and Motion we call Life.

A Life that is not formed out of Lies and Deception which causes conditions of confusion, which serve as evidence that such a quality of Life is not of the Divine Essence Making, and is lacking of its Divine Spirituality.

Aloneness Is Divine And Loneliness is A Curse Against The Spirit Of The Divine Being

Alone is the Sanctuary Of The Divine Essence (GOD) but loneliness is the prison of a profane Mind, which produce the spirit of lies and deceit, always attempting to attract the attention of the Divine, so as to Tempt and provoke the world to believe all that a lonely mind can not see and know that which is Divinely True and Real in and beyond life.

You can not become obsessed with Divine Truth and Reality when your mind is in a state of loneliness, but alone, the Mind is capable of taking you into the aloneness of infinity, there is where the mystery of Divine Truth and Reality is there to be discovered and to be known and not believed.

Alone, the Divine Essence reveals the myriad of all things physical, equipping those things with Divine Intelligence and gives those things of Matter, the ability to reason intelligent with a Divine Soul.

Yet giving all things with a physical life the ability to choose, and with a Will to act, in accordance to the status of the Mind of all living animate Beings.

So alone in your state of mental isolation, you are capable of harnessing Divine information, that which graduate the Divine Mind to discover and unravel the mysteries of the Universe, assigning no limitation to the Divine Essence, the Soul of the Infinite Divine Darkness, in and of which there from emerge all things intelligent designed, by the Alone Action of the Divine Essence.

So to be alone in Divine thought is to be in the company of the Divine Essence, the GOD Of Infinity, clothed in the infinite of the Perfect Night, the Space without illumination, but is the Mother and Father of such a display that bring Divine information into mental focus, to be known and understood.

It is the Divine Mind alone that guide you into the abyss of Divine Enlightenment about all things Divine, equipping you with a Divine intelligence that will qualify you to become wise in the decisions that you will make for your Body Life.

Loneliness is a handicap that prison the Mind and will have you to be confuse about who you are, having no knowledge of what the Divine Essence (GOD) is, and will have you speaking through belief, all things disrespectful about the Divine Infinite Darkness, and will even have you acting a clown while displaying your self to be ignorantly intelligent, while speaking evil about the Self that you do not know, and lying and deceiving all others about the Divine Essence Of All Things Physical And Nonphysical.

To be lonely in Life, is a Curse upon the Mind, preventing it from being qualified to Divinely Reason Rationally with Logic about the Cause and Effect that have your Mind to be in a lonely state, being nonfunctional on the realm of Divine intelligence, and the absent of such a mental gift, reveal a foolish mind, making claim through ignorant intelligence, to believe all that is not known in such a mental state of loneliness.

Many people today operate with a lonely mind and such a Mind produce mental illness that cause a psychotic spiritual reaction and with a lonely mind there can not be Divine Spiritual action, in protecting the self of your Body Life.

So there is no wonder why it is that most people in the world is in the state of Mental condition they are in today, and we show no desire to Divinely Change the present condition of the Body Life Living condition, today.

Loneliness produce the product of low self esteem, sadness, paranoid schizophrenic, a lack of self shame, anger without just cause, unhappiness, not joyful, complacency, idle mind, acts of deceit, docility, a lack of being aggressive for your own life protection and loneliness is to surrender to a slave spirit, such is the description of many people today.

HEALING

Much has been said and made claim of in the name of Healing, and there are many types of suggestion been given to you to be used in order to be able to experience a Healing process to those of you who from Time to Time is in need of a Body Healing to take place with you.

So anybody is claiming to be in need of Healing, which experience a body action which indicate that there is an interruption of the normal Divine Function within your body that is affecting the body organ and is causing pain, which prevent the body organs from functioning in Harmony, Order, and Balance, in relationship to all of your body organs.

So when there is an interruption of the organic equilibrium within your body, such serve as a sign that your body is in need of a Healing to take place within you.

There are all sorts of Quacks out there in the world claiming to be a Healer and they have been successful in convincing you that if something is wrong with your body function, then they are the Healer that can have your pain, and your ailment to disappear.

I am here to share with you that there can be nothing so deceiving than someone coming to you claiming to be able to heal your body and cause your ailment to be no more.

I will never claim to you to be a Healer, even though I am in constant pursuit of reaching the pinnacle of my Divine potential, which is to become Divinely Spiritual in the living of my Body Life.

Yet I will inform you of your ability to bring Healing to your self body, when ever it is experiencing the agony of discomfort, and that is what this book, Divine Spirituality is about, and I desire that it will serve as a guide to you in your effort to be Heal, both Spiritual and physically, should such an occasion of need, is to ever occur in your Body Life.

Healing your body when it is experiencing discomfort and Pain, or when your Body has been diagnosed with an illness that has the potential to threaten the continuation of your Life, as you would desire it to be, or stand not to be at all, meaning that Death is in the act to your life, such then will require you to act for the purpose of self healing.

The Greatest and Primary Healer to your Body Life, when such an action is in need for your Body to experience, the healer happens to be your self.

Because only you the patient, is capable of Healing your self, because all Healing process begin not by that someone claiming to be a Healer for you, it start with you, and it is the quality of your Mind Thoughts that serve as your Body Life Healer, because all things pertaining to your Body Life, begin with your Mind Thoughts.

You see, it is the thoughts emanating from your Mind that is capable of Healing what is ailing your Body Life, because only you are capable of directing the Divine Energy that is capable of correcting the problem that is within your Body Life, which is more Time than not.

Many things can cause an interruption of a function of a body organ that no longer is functioning in Harmony, Order, And Balance in relationship with your Body organs.

So, where there is no Harmony, Order, and Balance in the action that is going on within your Body Life, then that is what give way for those agents who are prone to adversely have an effect on the Divine action of your Body Organs, and if not corrected, it will bring pain and discomfort to your Body Life, even unto Death.

There is not one thing that is pertained to the Body Life that is more important to your Body Life physical action and how it is to function, than your Mind.

That is why it is your Mind Thoughts that must Function Divinely at all Time, in order to live a Divine Free Life that is Free from Pain and Disease.

Only you are capable of having your Mind to Think Divinely about your Self and the more Divine your Thoughts are the more Liberating your Life will happen to become.

Therefore, it is the quality of your Spirit that has an affect on the quality of Life you will experience and if you are not functioning in your Body Life with a Divine Spirit, then you open your Body Life to become susceptible for all kind of Disease to come into your Body Life Organs.

That is why this book is all about Divine Spirituality and is not about belief, because it take knowing who you are in order to be able to function in Life Divinely.

It is Divine Thoughts that are required in order for you to live a Divine Life and with such a Divine Spirit guiding your life, then the need for your Body Life to have a need for Healing, will be of no factor to your Life.

Healing is not about you needing somebody other than your self to lay hand upon the area of your body that is ailing your Body Life.

Healing is about you being qualified to place your Mind Thoughts on the area in need of healing, because it is in that Divine Spirit of Knowing, that will send the Divine healing Energy to heal that which is ailing your Body Life.

Because the quality of your thoughts can and will bring about a healing experience to your Body Life, and even when the surgeon go into your body to correct a problem within, it is your Mind that does the Healing, without it functioning in full confidence to that which is being performed within your body, you end up suffering the consequence of your lack of Mental discipline, concerning your self.

That is why it is very important for you to Know Thyself, over the course of your Body Life Living.

Even when others come to you, making claim to be a healer for you, and they proceed to lay hand upon you and pray for you, it must be you with your Mind of Divine Thought meditation to do the act of healing, displaying your Divine Spirituality.

Divine Spirituality is absent of belief, faith, and hope, but is in the Divine Spirit of Knowing that which you desire of your self in time of need to be heal, which will be accomplished only if you are in control of your Divine Mind thoughts.

The Spirit is all about the quality of your attitudinal behavior and is not about some ghostly ethereal mist floating around you, it is about the Ethereal Divine Energy that encapsulates your Body Life, making it possible for you to become your own healer in time of need.

When in time of need for self healing, you need isolation and an environment that bring nothing but consolation and assurance to your Divine Mind, so that only Divine Thoughts are present in the act of self healing.

Such is what allow your Divine Thoughts to become your Divine energy laser beam, as you direct such Divine thoughts to the area affected and is causing you pain and discomfort.

Only those with Divine Thoughts, need to be in your presence during the time of healing meditation, because Divine Thoughts beget Divine Thoughts and they all must be concentrated on the same target, if healing is to take place with you.

So that you all will become as One Divine Mind, because Divinity beget Divinity, when the atmosphere is of one accord in Divine Thought.

When in your Divine Mind, it require no set ritual to be performed other than your Divine meditation of Divine

Thoughts, directed to become the healing source that will bring about a healing process to your ailing Body Life.

There need not be any loud praying, chanting, jumping up and down calling on any and everybody that you have been conditioned to believe is your healing source, all you need is the discipline of Divine Thought, directed to your self that is in need of healing, because it is the Divine Energy of your thoughts that serve as your healing power and you being the healer of your Body life, when such is ever needed

I come and I share with you, not that which is conventional but that which is unconventional and not believable, but is thoughtful creative, in the process of healing your body life ailment.

9 781440 176050